Keep your customers
(and keep them happy)

Keep your customers

(and keep them happy)

Stanley J. Fenvessy

DOW JONES-IRWIN Homewood, Illinois 60430

First Printing, April 1976

ISBN 0-87094-120-8
Library of Congress Catalog Card No. 75–43168
Printed in the United States of America

Preface

This book is your guide to developing and maintaining good communications with your customers. The theme is that organization is the secret to efficient and effective communications with your customers. The money you spend on training your sales staff and on advertising programs will be wasted if you can't respond quickly to the queries, complaints, and suggestions of those who do, or want to do, business with you. It is my hope that this book will provide you with the information you need to "keep your customers, and keep them happy."

Acknowledgments

First and foremost I wish to acknowledge the invaluable aid of my friend, David E. Schaffer of Franconia, New Hampshire, in writing Chapter 3, Burgeoning Legal Requirements That Generate Customer Communications. In addition, I am grateful to my clients and other companies who agreed to the inclusion of forms and other illustrations that are so useful in making plain just what it is that has to be done. I also wish to acknowledge the aid of my staff at Fenvessy Associates, Inc., and in particular Robert F. Bonner for his assistance in the preparation of the illustrations and my secretary, Virginia vi

Yager, who was so persevering and helpful in typing and then retyping this manuscript so many times. My good friend, Mel Mandell, was of inestimable help in preparing this manuscript for publication. Finally, I wish to express my deep appreciation to my wife, Doris, for her patience and understanding in allowing me to devote so many of our weekends to this task.

March 1976   STANLEY J. FENVESSY

Contents

An inexpensive substitute for market and service research. De-layed counterpunching. A communications system not costly. Reinforcing the free enterprise system.

Detecting the partially satisfactory response system: *A standard for comparison.*

"Clear and conspicuous": *Consumer Products Safety Commission. Consumer Office of the President. The role of Congress. The Federal Reserve Board.* Other important developments.

Organizations meriting priority: *The expanding Federal Trade Commission. The U.S. Postal Service. The Better Business Bureau. Attorneys general and other governmental consumer advocates. "Action lines" popular in broadcasting. DMMA and its "action line." Trade associations. Attorneys representing the individual customer. When the courts intervene. Important distributors and dealers.* The significance of "consumerism": *The future of consumerism.*

Responding—formal and informal: *Processing responses. Direct handling.* Test yourself.

List of illustrations

chapter 1

Why improved communications with customers are so important today

Because present customers are and always will be our best prospects.

This is far and away the overriding reason why all companies should develop and maintain superior—not merely "good" —communications with customers. Efficient and informative communications also impress *future* customers—prospects who request the company's literature and catalogs, or who merely contact the company to find out how the company's products can be ordered and where they are available in the prospect's locality.

Beyond these major inducements to top-notch communications, there are lesser but important inducements. First among these is the growing pressure from all sorts of organizations, mainly governmental, to respond promptly and equitably to the complaints of the consumer. No businessman needs to be

1

told that consumerism is a powerful force, one not likely to subside. The best way to deal with consumerism is to "get organized."

Organizing doesn't mean surrendering to unreasonable demands. Rather, it means taking steps to convince the consumer that you genuinely have his or her interest at heart and are not playing the role of adversary.

One simple way to gain the customer's confidence is to make it easy for him to communicate. As the Sub-Council on Complaints and Remedies of the President's National Business Council for Consumer Affairs stated on page 5 of its report, entitled *Complaints and Remedies,*[1] ". . . sellers should take steps to inform consumers about available channels for complaint and redress; a complaint unregistered is no less significant in the harm it creates than a complaint mishandled or unresolved."

A number of years ago, J. C. Penney Company, Inc., took one obvious step toward expediting customer complaints: The procedure for returning unwanted merchandise or complaining, and the address to which the merchandise and the complaint should be sent, are spelled out on every packing slip accompanying mail-order merchandise (see Figure 1). This was considered a radical and foolhardy step at the time. Many people felt that it would markedly increase merchandise returns, thereby causing additional expense. However, the tests made then, and those repeated since, have shown skeptics that this innovation does not increase returns or complaints, and, because the customer is instructed what to do, the transaction can be handled faster and more economically.

---

[1] This informative 16-page brochure is available for 70 cents from the Superintendent of Documents, U.S. Government Printing Office, Washington, D.C. 20402.

FIGURE 1

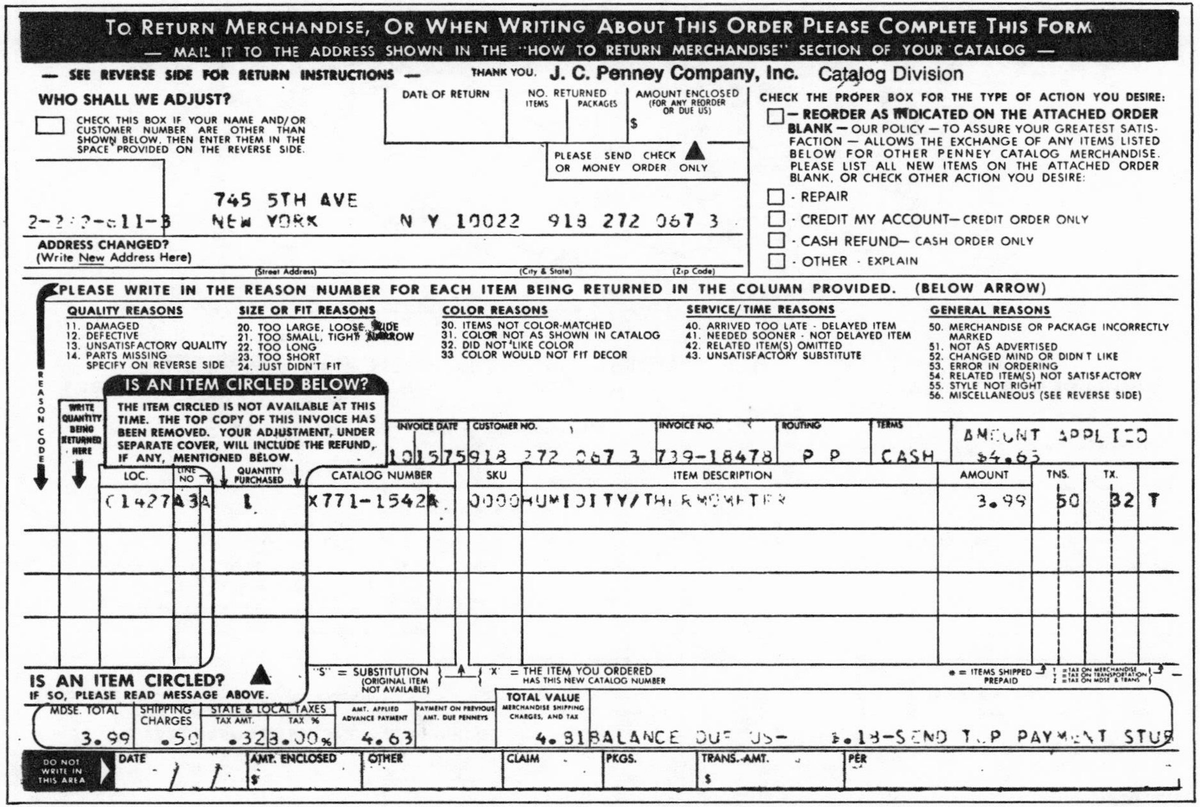

TO RETURN MERCHANDISE, OR WHEN WRITING ABOUT THIS ORDER PLEASE COMPLETE THIS FORM
— MAIL IT TO THE ADDRESS SHOWN IN THE "HOW TO RETURN MERCHANDISE" SECTION OF YOUR CATALOG —

— SEE REVERSE SIDE FOR RETURN INSTRUCTIONS — THANK YOU. J. C. Penney Company, Inc. Catalog Division

WHO SHALL WE ADJUST?

CHECK THIS BOX IF YOUR NAME AND/OR CUSTOMER NUMBER ARE OTHER THAN SHOWN BELOW, THEN ENTER THEM IN THE SPACE PROVIDED ON THE REVERSE SIDE.

DATE OF RETURN | NO. RETURNED ITEMS | PACKAGES | AMOUNT ENCLOSED (FOR ANY REORDER OR DUE US) $

PLEASE SEND CHECK OR MONEY ORDER ONLY

745 5TH AVE
2-2·?-c11-3 NEW YORK N Y 10022 913 272 067 3

ADDRESS CHANGED?
(Write New Address Here)
(Street Address) (City & State) (Zip Code)

CHECK THE PROPER BOX FOR THE TYPE OF ACTION YOU DESIRE:
- REORDER AS INDICATED ON THE ATTACHED ORDER BLANK — OUR POLICY — TO ASSURE YOUR GREATEST SATISFACTION — ALLOWS THE EXCHANGE OF ANY ITEMS LISTED BELOW FOR OTHER PENNEY CATALOG MERCHANDISE. PLEASE LIST ALL NEW ITEMS ON THE ATTACHED ORDER BLANK, OR CHECK OTHER ACTION YOU DESIRE:
- REPAIR
- CREDIT MY ACCOUNT— CREDIT ORDER ONLY
- CASH REFUND— CASH ORDER ONLY
- OTHER · EXPLAIN

PLEASE WRITE IN THE REASON NUMBER FOR EACH ITEM BEING RETURNED IN THE COLUMN PROVIDED. (BELOW ARROW)

QUALITY REASONS
11. DAMAGED
12. DEFECTIVE
13. UNSATISFACTORY QUALITY
14. PARTS MISSING
SPECIFY ON REVERSE SIDE

SIZE OR FIT REASONS
20. TOO LARGE, LOOSE, WIDE
21. TOO SMALL, TIGHT NARROW
22. TOO LONG
23. TOO SHORT
24. JUST DIDN'T FIT

COLOR REASONS
30. ITEMS NOT COLOR-MATCHED
31. COLOR NOT AS SHOWN IN CATALOG
32. DID NOT LIKE COLOR
33 COLOR WOULD NOT FIT DECOR

SERVICE/TIME REASONS
40. ARRIVED TOO LATE - DELAYED ITEM
41. NEEDED SOONER - NOT DELAYED ITEM
42. RELATED ITEM(S) OMITTED
43. UNSATISFACTORY SUBSTITUTE

GENERAL REASONS
50. MERCHANDISE OR PACKAGE INCORRECTLY MARKED
51. NOT AS ADVERTISED
52. CHANGED MIND OR DIDN T LIKE
53. ERROR IN ORDERING
54. RELATED ITEM(S) NOT SATISFACTORY
55. STYLE NOT RIGHT
56. MISCELLANEOUS (SEE REVERSE SIDE)

REASON CODE | WRITE QUANTITY BEING RETURNED HERE

IS AN ITEM CIRCLED BELOW?
THE ITEM CIRCLED IS NOT AVAILABLE AT THIS TIME. THE TOP COPY OF THIS INVOICE HAS BEEN REMOVED. YOUR ADJUSTMENT, UNDER SEPARATE COVER, WILL INCLUDE THE REFUND, IF ANY, MENTIONED BELOW.

INVOICE DATE	CUSTOMER NO.	INVOICE NO.	ROUTING	TERMS	
101575	913 272 067 3	739-18478	P P	CASH	AMOUNT APPLIED $4.63

LOC.	LINE NO	QUANTITY PURCHASED	CATALOG NUMBER	SKU	ITEM DESCRIPTION	AMOUNT	TNS.	TX.
C1427	A3A	1	X771-1542A	0000	HUMIDITY/THERMOMETER	3.99	50	32 T

IS AN ITEM CIRCLED?
IF SO, PLEASE READ MESSAGE ABOVE.

"S" = SUBSTITUTION (ORIGINAL ITEM NOT AVAILABLE) "X" = THE ITEM YOU ORDERED HAS THIS NEW CATALOG NUMBER
• = ITEMS SHIPPED PREPAID 1 = TAX ON MERCHANDISE 2 = TAX ON TRANSPORTATION 3 = TAX ON MDSE & TRANS

MDSE. TOTAL	SHIPPING CHARGES	STATE & LOCAL TAXES TAX AMT.	TAX %	AMT. APPLIED ADVANCE PAYMENT	PAYMENT ON PREVIOUS AMT. DUE PENNEYS	TOTAL VALUE MERCHANDISE SHIPPING CHARGES, AND TAX	
3.99	.50	.32	3.00%	4.63		4.81	BALANCE DUE US- $.18-SEND T.P PAYMENT STUB

DO NOT WRITE IN THIS AREA	DATE	AMT. ENCLOSED	OTHER	CLAIM	PKGS.	TRANS.-AMT.	PER
	/ /	$				$	

Front of form included with goods shipped by J. C. Penney Company, Inc., telling the customer how to properly prepare exchanges and returns. Enclosing this form has not resulted in an increase in returns.

FIGURE 1 *(continued)*

DEAR CUSTOMER: To obtain a prompt and complete adjustment, please complete the reverse side and follow instructions as outlined below.

IF YOUR NAME AND/OR CUSTOMER NUMBER IS OTHER THAN THAT SHOWN ON THE REVERSE SIDE OF THIS FORM— PLEASE ENTER CORRECTED INFORMATION HERE:

YOUR PENNEY
CUSTOMER NUMBER ▶ □□□□□□□□

NAME _____ ADDRESS _____ CITY AND STATE _____ ZIP CODE _____

IF YOU ARE EXCHANGING OR RETURNING MERCHANDISE:

Because "YOUR SATISFACTION IS OUR GOAL," we need your help. To insure greater satisfaction for your future orders, please write the code in the column provided on the reverse side which most closely corresponds to the reason for this return. If it is necessary to further explain, or if the reason is Miscellaneous, please write your comments here:

_____

_____

(IF MORE SPACE IS REQUIRED, ATTACH A SEPARATE PIECE OF PAPER.)

DAMAGED IN TRANSIT:
1 If merchandise delivered by Parcel Post is damaged on arrival, fill out the reverse side of this form and send it to us along with the merchandise.

2 If merchandise delivered by REA-Express or Truck is damaged on arrival, obtain an Inspection Report from the driver and have him take the package back. (If you discover the damage after the delivery driver has left, notify the carrier, who will then pick up the package and give you the Inspection Report.) Send us the Inspection Report, the paid transportation bill, and this completed form.

EXCHANGE OR REFUND
1 If you are returning merchandise for any reason other than damaged in transit and it can be returned by Parcel Post, simply fill out this form and send it to us with the merchandise.

2 If it is necessary to return merchandise by freight or express, write us first for instructions. Fill out this form and give us the details regarding your return. Upon receipt of your correspondence, we will tell you how and where to return the merchandise.

The proper address to forward any correspondence or merchandise that you wish to return is shown in the "HOW TO RETURN MERCHANDISE" section of your catalog.

ENCLOSE THE FOLLOWING IN YOUR PACKAGE:

● THIS RETURN FORM

● ANY NECESSARY CORRESPONDENCE

IF RETURNED VIA PARCEL POST APPLY THE PROPER POSTAGE FOR PACKAGE PLUS 1st CLASS POSTAGE IF THERE IS A LETTER OR OTHER CORRESPONDENCE ENCLOSED

FIRST CLASS ENCLOSED

J.C. PENNEY CO.
Catalog D.
City, State, Zip Code

YOUR RETURN ADDRESS

SEE "HOW TO RETURN MDSE." SECTION OF YOUR CATALOG FOR PROPER ADDRESS

Reverse of the J. C. Penney form.

FIGURE 2

American Express Company
Card Div

FOR HELP WITH ANY PROBLEM OR QUESTION ABOUT
YOUR ACCOUNT, CALL 212-677-5500

Listing of Charges and Credits

Account No. — Page 01 of 01

Card No.	Reference No.	Listing of Charges and Credits	Charges	Credits
100	032270	LINCROFT INN LINCROFT NJ	1908	
100	265270	CHARGE RECORD ENCLOSED	2996	
000	835278	REMITTANCE - PAYMENT RECEIVED THANK YOU		88736
100	034288	WRIGHT ARCH PRESERVERS NEW YORK NY	5850	
100	127294	THE PLAZA NEW YORK NY	2215	
100	024296	HARVEYS RSTR WASHINGTON DC	5700	
100	033298	LOEWS LENFANT WASHINGTON DC	6061	
100	691298	EASTERN AIRLINES INC 295	29400	
101	050294	MADISON AVE FLORIST NEW YORK NY	1700	
		PAGE TOTAL	55830	88736
		ACCOUNT TOTAL	55830	88736

Please see reverse side for
information regarding certain types of charges

Billing Date
10/28

An example of a monthly statement that provides a phone number for easier customer communication.

Many hundreds of companies use the inward-WATS service of the telephone companies to expedite customer contacts. It's now becoming quite common to see an "800" number listed in ads or to have it included in commercials on radio and TV. The use of inward-WATS service is detailed in Chapter 10.

Also, to assist customers, many firms include on their order acknowledgements or invoices the name of an executive or a post office box number, or both, or a telephone number[2] where customer inquiries or complaints should be directed to obtain

---

[2] Among the charges made in a 37-page "Complaint" filed late in 1975 by the Federal Trade Commission against a mail-order house with a long record of misrepresentation is that the company had an unlisted phone number. If the complaint is upheld it will require that the company in question ". . . shall maintain a business telephone number and shall list such number in the official telephone directory for its location and in all of its mail order catalogs and advertisements." The Direct Mail/Marketing Association (see Chapter 4) reports that it is quite common for mail-order houses to have unlisted phones.

special attention. The Credit Card Division of American Express Company pioneered in this direction. Figure 2 is an example of their monthly statement providing a telephone number for easier communication.

AN INEXPENSIVE SUBSTITUTE FOR MARKET AND SERVICE RESEARCH

There are other good reasons for effective handling of customer contacts: The responses, if properly compiled and analyzed, give the astute marketer an insight into the real and even the future needs of the customer. Conversely, one should be able to determine which of the company's "mature" products are in need of an upgrading on the basis of customer responses. The company's designers should also be privy to the compiled responses, which may help them to concentrate on some hitherto unrevealed deficiencies of products and to eliminate these faults as much as possible.

The compiled responses can also point up shortcomings in order fulfillment. Order processing delays, incorrect order filling, slow deliveries by carriers, damage, and inadequate assembly and operating instructions are frequently highlighted in customer mail. Regularly compiled summaries of this data should be invaluable to alert operating management.

The customer mail also serves to educate whomever in the company is responsible for supervising customer communications (in large companies this executive often has the title of director of consumer affairs). Thus, when a new product or service is planned, this executive should be exposed to the new product or service concept and be asked to play the devil's advocate. Presumably, with his or her heightened sensitivity to the customer's needs, he or she (in companies whose products are designed for women, the executive should be a woman) should offer useful insights into the probable reception the new product will be given. Or, he or she could offer some intelligent suggestions on how to improve the new product. In view of the high cost of introducing new products and services, every such avenue towards eliminating failure in the marketplace should be explored.

DELAYED COUNTERPUNCHING

Unfortunately, too many companies wait too long to establish meaningful policies and efficient systems for dealing with customers. As a result, they are *pushed* into setting up a response mechanism. It is bad enough to be stung into action by the lashes of consumerists. Even worse, a company may be stampeded into taking this needed step because major competitors have set up highly efficient response systems that are winning the accolades—and loyalty—of the consumer. When this happens, or rather when the laggard firm senses that it is losing out to competition, extra-costly expediting may be needed to catch up. That is, if it can ever catch up!—because the company that gains a solid reputation for quick, friendly, and truthful communications with the consumer may seize a lead that no force-fed efforts can close.

There's another situation in which companies are pushed belatedly into upgrading their customer communications: when the morale of sales personnel declines because good customers resent the lack of prompt and personal responsiveness on the part of the company. If a company waits that long, its management may need upgrading, too.

Sometimes, a traumatic incident jabs management into improving the response system. Don't wait until Ralph Nader or Consumers Union castigates you publicly, or until the local newspaper columnist or radio or TV "Action Line" exposes your company's deficiencies—customer service.

A COMMUNICATIONS SYSTEM IS NOT COSTLY

No company should be deterred because of cost from setting up an effective system for handling customer contacts. Aside from the obvious fact that such a system "pays for itself" in increased customer satisfaction and sales, the actual out-of-pocket costs of a system may actually be less than what a company now expends on a second-rate system that antagonizes customers.

"Less costly! How can this be true?" The answer is that companies with effective systems hold down the costs by such basic measures as these:

Providing the customer with explicit instructions on what to do if there is a problem.

Using properly selected, trained, and motivated personnel.

Answering customers promptly, thus eliminating follow-up calls and letters.

Not devoting valuable office space and time to filing customer correspondence, unless it is of the "exceptionally aggrieved" nature.

Adopting appropriate and explicit form letters and form postcards for responses, instead of typing individual letters.

Maintaining records on both the departmental and individual

productivity that guide management in raising efficiency.
Apply mechanization and automation only where they are cost
effective.

Using the telephone to handle complicated problems.

Employing the expertise of consultants and of the company
executives in charge of customer communications to modify
company advertising, catalogs, order forms, and other promotional material in a way that helps eliminate unneeded
customer communications. (How this is done is detailed in
Chapter 5.)

Finally, the costs of responding to customers should be lowered by concentrating this activity in one place under one
knowledgeable, trained executive so that customer correspondence is not shuffled about the company from department to
department. Otherwise, too many employees will be wasting
time trying to figure out how to respond—and perhaps not
responding at all, or very late, which is practically as bad.

REINFORCING THE FREE
ENTERPRISE SYSTEM

If and when your company upgrades its response system,
it will be making a less tangible but long-range contribution
to its own welfare. No need to tell you that the free enterprise
system is under attack on many fronts. Now *we* know that our
capitalistic system is much more responsive to the needs of the
consumer than any other system. But few Americans have any
experience with the rigidity of socialistic, communistic, or
ostensibly capitalistic yet tightly planned economies of other
nations. Many don't realize how poorly they would fare under

such controlled economies. In being not alert to the deficiencies of the alternatives to free enterprise, they are all too ready to believe the worst about American companies and those who direct them.

By setting up responsive, equitable systems for dealing with customers, your company helps generate needed confidence in the economy of the United States. We need that assurance.

chapter 2

How to tell if you have a problem

Returned merchandise is enclosed in a large package that also contains the sender's garbage.

The complainer works in a computer department, so he or she prepares the complaint in the form of a stack of punched cards that must be fed into a computer for translation into plain language.

The complainer makes many photocopies of his original complaint and sends in one each day until he obtains a satisfactory answer.

Cartridges are enclosed in the envelope with instructions to the president of the company to "blow his head off."

Extraordinary! Pranks? Or the expression of unbalanced people? Perhaps. Or are these the desperate measures taken by customers who just can't seem to trigger a response by more polite communications?

If your company receives communications of this nature, you should take heed. What are some of the other signs indicating that your company is doing a poor job of responding to customers, beyond those suggested in the previous chapter (i.e., falling sales, lowered morale of sales personnel, and divided responsibility)?

When the president or other senior officers of the company are assailed with phone calls, letters, and telegrams from irate customers—take action.

If important reps, dealers, and distributors drop your retail lines, check to find out if poor response to their customers' complaints was one of the unarticulated reasons for the divorce.

If the response rate to your latest catalog or direct mail or phone promotion is lower than for previous offers, check the backlog in your customer service department.

If the credit department is experiencing collection problems, investigate whether payments are being withheld because of unresolved customer service problems.

Of course, there is another sure sign of deficiency: when the company begins to receive a lot of complaints directly from such VIPs (discussed in Chapter 4) as the Federal Trade Commission, Postal Service, state attorneys general, Better Business Bureau, and trade associations, and the "Action Lines" set up by newspapers, broadcasting stations, and the Direct Mail/ Marketing Association.

DETECTING THE PARTIALLY SATISFACTORY RESPONSE SYSTEM

When a company is doing a really poor job of handling customer contacts, it becomes obvious quickly—and to even the most casual observer. However, what about the company that has set up a response system, perhaps some years ago, and complacently believes that it is doing a good job? How does a company in this situation determine if it is doing a good job?

There are many ways. One is to compare your own response mechanism to that of well-managed companies whose response systems are deemed exceptional or highly effective. (And don't just compare your system with those of companies in the same industry; check other industries as well.) There are many standards by which you can judge whether or not your system is up to snuff.

1. Turnaround time on written communications. Customers should receive a response during the calendar week following the week they mailed their letters. This leaves, at most, two to three working days to read, research, and respond.

2. Answering telephone calls. Phone calls should be answered within 24 hours. In truly effective operations, calls are resolved while the customer is on the line, so the company does not have to bear the additional expense of a return call.

3. The ratio between orders or subscribers and "contacts." For example, one major mail-order operation expects to receive four customer communications per 100 orders. The publisher of a well-run magazine looks for subscriber mail each year equivalent to 4 percent of his subscription list.

4. The ratio of clerks to contacts. In a very efficient operation, this ratio is one clerk to 280 contacts per week. How does your company compare?

5. The approach to or level of technology. For example, whether clerks are still typing individual letters when form letters or automatic typing or handwritten replies would be just as satisfactory to the customer—and be much faster and less costly.

6. When a consultant or executive of a company with which yours has had good relations and is experienced in response systems, surveys your system and indicates valid reasons why

it is not on a par with that of competitive companies or is otherwise deficient. (However, if that consultant recommends a great investment in equipment, seek a second opinion.)

7. When your dealers pointedly compliment a competitor on the effectiveness of his response system.

8. If you make a big investment in electronic data processing (EDP), word processing, or automatic typing equipment, but response time to customer complaints does not decline. (One company installed an elaborate computer terminal system for retrieving microfilm copies of the originals of customer orders in hopes of improving service. Months later, to management's chagrin, it found there had been no improvement at all in response time; the problem was in approach, not technology.)

A standard for comparison

There are other characteristics of effective customer service operations. These examples should help you determine if your operations measure up:

Customers rarely if ever follow up an initial communication with a second letter of complaint—although they may write to compliment individual clerks or the company for the prompt handling of the initial complaint.

A very low percentage of customer communications are addressed to the chairman, president, or other officers of the corporation.

The customer service department is neat, desks are orderly, and the department visually appears well organized.

Overtime work is minimal.

Turnover among the clerks handling customer service is low, indicating that these employees are well motivated and supervised, and are generally happy in their work.

Work backlog does not exceed two to three days. The oldest letter on hand (and that, usually, is one waiting for special information) is not over seven days old.

Because customers are satisfied by the company's response to their initial communication, they rarely if ever turn for redress to the various consumer-advocacy organizations. As a result, the company receives only a rare communication from such organizations as the FTC, BBB, or the Postal Service. (To expect no contacts whatsoever from consumer advocates is unrealistic because there is a small number of highly neurotic or militant cranks or outright frauds who can never be satisfied by a reasonable policy of redress.)

There is a high level of repeat orders from loyal customers.

The sales service staff has developed such expertise in picking substitutes when the customer's original choice is out of stock that returns of these substitutes falls to a very low level.

Sales representatives have no complaints about customer service at sales meetings.

Customer service expense is decreasing as a percent of sales as the company sales volume increases.

The customer service department receives many more than the heretofore rare and yellowed complimentary letter thumbtacked on the bulletin board of the company with problems.

chapter 3

Burgeoning legal requirements that generate customer communications

No business executive needs to be told that there is a vast body of law affecting his or her relations with consumers —and that this great mass of law and regulation is growing all the time. In fact, a leading reference book on consumer affairs and customer relations includes no less than 12,000 references. To summarize all of them is obviously beyond the scope of a single chapter. That's why an *attitude* is offered here for businessmen to adopt that will help them to cope with *all* the regulations. In addition, some useful sources of up-to-date information on these laws is given.

There are two main categories of regulation. These are:

1. *Regulations directly concerned with advertising.* It is obvious, when a purchase of goods or services is stimulated by an advertisement, that the customer will expect to receive for his money what is promised in the ad, whether that promise is by direct statement or by implication. There are many specific regulations on the federal, state, and local governmental levels concerning this important aspect of advertising. The regulations

define such concepts as what is a fact when a fact is disclosed in an ad, and they further define the "impressions" that the customer may receive from the ad. By establishing such regulations, the various governments make mandatory fair advertising that limits disappointment. Obviously, advertising is an important element in customer relations.

2. *Regulations directly related to customer relations.* There are numerous federal, state, and municipal regulations concerned with the "deal" that the customer makes when purchasing a service or product. They are not concerned so much with the product, but rather with the business relationship the customer has established with the seller as a result of his purchase. These regulations as such are concerned with product warranty, payment, credit investigation, complaint handling, and many other aspects of customer relations.

"CLEAR AND CONSPICUOUS"

The basic concept that underlies all advertising law (particularly those laws and regulations mentioned in the preceding Category 1) is that an ad should create for the "average man" an impression of the product for sale that this product or service will live up to a certain standard. Facts should be accurate and impressions should be reasonable. Thus, the act of delaying presentation of the truth till the last page of a multipage promotional brochure, or of creating a false impression on the front page, is against the law. Creating an overly "puffed" impression in a headline, and disclaiming that impression in small print below, is against the law. Facts should be presented so clearly and conspicuously that the buyer knows what he is buying and knows the nature of his ongoing relationship with the seller. Puffery (the exaggeration of the virtues of a product or service) is legal, but only if the exaggerated image does not overwhelm the common sense of the average man.

It is important to note that all regulatory agencies operate on a complaint basis. They seldom will move against a company even for an ad that violates the "clear-and-conspicuous" rule, unless they receive a substantial number of complaints from consumers as to the unfairness or inaccuracy of the ad that stimulated purchase.

Many times some difficulty can arise from the false impression that an ad creates. If the seller's customer relations department is on its toes, by properly reviewing the ad prior to publication it can mitigate the situation and prevent a damaging action against the company by a regulatory authority. If, however, a complaint is made by a regulatory authority, the judgment of that authority as to the truth or falseness of the ad is made not only by ascertaining the factual clearness of the advertisement, but takes into consideration the impact of the advertisement as a whole. This whole concerns art and layout as well as words—the relative weight of headline versus body copy, the size of the ad, the clarity of the disclosure, the aura created by puffery, and numerous other factors.

The regulatory authorities know full well that most customer complaints do not concern some specific detail, but actually arise from an intentional or unintentional gap between the advertised product or service and the actual delivered product or service.

Referring to Category 2, above, which is about those laws and regulations concerned directly with customer relations, the same principles hold effect as those that are concerned with advertising. Here the contractual relationship between the buyer and seller is defined. Since the buyer is buying not only a product but a relationship, there should be no unfairness or lack of clarity in the description of the deal. All too often, sellers fail to maintain the most rudimentary relationship with the consumer after purchase. Thus, regulations as to billing practices, dunning, warranty, and complaint handling make the seller comply with a basic fairness in a relationship with the customer.

All in all, the key word is *equity*. The trend of governmental regulation is clear. It has resulted from a recent disintegration in the buyer-seller relationship. Equity means reasonable fairness, and all businessmen should acquaint themselves with the laws and regulations concerning their business.

All three governmental levels regulate the areas of activity of business concerned with customer relations.

1. *Federal Government*
   a. Federal Trade Commission.
   b. U.S. Postal Service.
   c. Consumer Products Safety Commission.
   d. Consumer Office of the President.
   e. The Congress.
   f. Federal Reserve Board.
2. *State Regulatory Authority*
   a. Attorney General's Department
   b. State Regulatory Agencies
3. *Local Regulatory Authority* (which can include county government as well).

(The roles of the Federal Trade Commission and the U.S. Postal Service are discussed in the next chapter.)

Consumer Products Safety Commission

The recently created Consumer Products Safety Commission (CPSC) deserves mention not because it is directly concerned with consumer relations, but because much of the information it needs concerning the safety of products sold throughout the United States will come through customer complaints. The seller should be very aware of reported hazards in the goods that they sell. Customer relations departments should be extremely sensitive to complaints related to the safety of the company's products. In addition, management must be highly aware of any regulation concerning their products that comes forth from the CPSC.

Consumer Office of the President

The Consumer Office of the President is largely a political and public relations arm of the office of the President. One of its major functions is to serve as a complaint clearinghouse; it often corresponds on an individual basis with alleged wrongdoers. One of the main reasons for being aware of its activities is that it serves as a spokesman for the President, and its pronouncements often foretell forthcoming legislative directions that the President will initiate or support.

The role of Congress

The Congress has increasingly in late years taken on the role of consumer protector. Recently it has addressed itself to some of the major consumer concerns. The Fair Credit Billing Act, the Fair Credit Reporting Act, and the Truth in Lending Regulation Z are only a few of the concerned or proposed laws.

The Federal Reserve Board

The Federal Reserve Board administers, together with the FTC, much of the credit regulation concerned with customer relations. It sets the rules and the FTC administers them.

OTHER IMPORTANT DEVELOPMENTS

Two recent trends are noteworthy in that they represent directions that the federal government is taking at this time regarding consumer regulations.

1. There is a possibility that a consumer agency will be set up as a major arm of the executive department. Many people and organizations have complained that the consumer has had no executive voice in governmental regulations and lawmaking. This new agency, which might be created by the Congress, will serve as an ombudsman for the consumer in a broad spectrum of matters. The agency will involve itself in lawmaking, classic suits in the behalf of the consumer, and, as well, take his part in hearings conducted for one reason or another by other federal agencies that are concerned with consumer matters. Articulate consumer advocates have pointed out, not without evidence, that too many federal agencies create regulations for the benefit of those regulated, and not on the behalf of the customers of those regulated. What is important is that this new agency, if it is created, would be very powerful, and it should be effective in moving against practices unfair to the consumer.

2. In the opposite direction, the members of the Federal Trade Commission have spoken out lately against the commission's practice of "taking action in small matters." Their belief is that the commission has spent too much of its time and money moving against companies for relatively unimportant

violations of FTC codes of ethics and practices. The effort now will be to move against only those practices that involve substantial harm to the consumer. Though this will relieve the oft-cited complaint by businessmen of harassment by the FTC, it will give the FTC time and money to move against those activities that really deserve its attention. Whereas business heretofore has been protected from the FTC by that agency's inefficiencies, this will no longer be the case. Together with new powers recently given to the FTC by the Supreme Court and the Congress, the FTC will be a highly effective arm against unclear advertising and unfair practices that hurt the consumer. The situation suggests the admonition "let the seller beware." What the seller must do is face clearly and honestly the practices in his business that are involved with customer relations, and if the seller, putting himself in the place of the consumer, finds those practices grossly unfair, they must be changed.

Here are a few kinds of rules and laws that are examples of what has been referred to in the preceding discussion.

A. *Laws and regulations directly concerned with advertising.* The FTC's regulation concerning the use of the word "free." This regulation prescribes the manner and means in which "free" can be used in connection with the sale of a product. Much of the thrust of the regulation goes towards detailing the manner in which any qualifications for the receipt of the free gift, or what have you, is stated and disclosed. The same regulation controls other gift situations, such as "1 cent sales" and the like.

B. *Laws and regulations directly pertinent to consumer relations.* Two examples can be cited here. The first is a *proposed* regulation *already enforced* by the Federal Trade

Commission through its consent procedures. This regulation administers the rules by which mail-order houses can delay delivery on an ordered item. In general, mail-order merchants are given 30 days to deliver. If delivery is delayed or prevented, certain notices must be sent to the customer giving that customer various options, including cancellation of the sale.

A second example of this type of regulation is the New York State law that controls the actions of a company confronted with a letter from a consumer claiming a billing error. The law prescribes the maximum amount of time by which the seller must answer such a complaint, and the additional period available to take adequate remedies to handle the consumer's concern.

A further example of this type of law and regulation is the FTC-Warranty Act recently passed by Congress. Here, the definition of implied warranty is made that says, essentially, that a product must serve the obvious purpose for which it was created. As silly as this seems, this statement prevents a company from failing to back a defective product. The law goes on to state in detail the manner and means in which warranty should be disclosed; it prevents companies from expressing warranties that are weaker than the implied warranty. There are, to support the law, many established cases in which the FTC, under its disclosure and unfairness doctrines, ruled against companies that abused and misused the whole notion of warranting their product.

In other areas, whole industries have been regulated under either example A or B above. An illustration of this is the negative-option regulation issued by the Federal Trade Commission a few years ago. Here, negative-option clubs (such as book and record clubs where merchandise is automatically mailed to a club member unless she or he indicates a wish not to receive it) were told precisely the scope and manner of their relationship with the consumer. This admonition is not only concerned with the factual disclosure necessary, but extends to stating just how the back-and-forth, day-to-day business of a club operates and should be conducted with its customers.

The Federal Trade Commission regulations also are concerned with the manner and means by which door-to-door salesmen and other direct sellers conduct their business. One of the most unusual facets of this regulation is the three-day cancellation privilege. In essence, it means that a direct-selling contract is not permanently valid when agreement and consideration take place, but only three days later, giving the customer time to change his mind.

There are regulations concerning the rules by which games and sweepstakes can be conducted in connection with sales. The FTC, in connection with the Federal Reserve Board, administers a very wide range of regulations over almost all extensions of open-ended and closed-ended consumer credit. This would take several books to describe, but some of the major highlights of credit regulation are: the Fair Credit Disclosure Act, which prescribes how the terms of the credit agreement must be disclosed; the Fair Credit Reporting Act, which regulates the flow of credit information throughout the commercial world; and the various lesser regulations controlling credit card practices, discrimination in credit extension, and so forth.

All of these acts, of course, are uniquely tied to consumer relations in that almost any complaint a customer may offer— such as the usual nondelivery/nonreceipt, "I have returned," and "I have paid"—are specifically related to one or another section of existing regulations. In the absence of specific knowledge regarding these regulations, the businessman can only retreat to common sense, and the directness of fairness and equity in his relationship with customers. Though it is not a law or rule, one could apply the Golden Rule and say that if the businessman treats the consumer as he would wish to be treated himself, he will not stray too far from doing what is right according to the law.

USEFUL PUBLICATIONS

Nevertheless, the law disregards ignorance of itself. To that effect, there are certain excellent sources of information of which businesspeople should avail themselves. The first of these, of course, is his or her attorney or company counsel. Next, the consumer relations or the governmental regulation departments of whatever trade association to which he or she may belong. In addition, two excellent publications of a semi-legal nature are available. These are not written in legal jargon but are readily understood by the layperson. The first is available from the Council of Better Business Bureaus, Inc., 1150 17th Street, N.W., Washington, D.C. 20036, and is called *Do's and Don'ts in Advertising Copy.* Though the title would imply that the publication is concerned with advertising, it also refers to all the rules and regulations concerned with customer relations when such rules have anything at all to do with advertising. *Do's and Don'ts in Advertising Copy* costs $150 for the first year's subscription and $50 for each year thereafter.

Another useful periodical is the *Anti-trust and Trade Regulation Report,* published by the Bureau of National Affairs, 1231 25th Street, N.W., Washington, D.C. 20037. This weekly report summarizes the various acts of regulatory authorities, mainly the Federal Trade Commission. Though it does not fully describe each action that the FTC takes, it does on a timely basis trigger an alarm to any concerned area. These weekly reports cost $256 for a one-year subscription and $246 per year on a two-year subscription.

In addition, there are numerous trade association newsletters such as *Consumer Trends,* published by International Consumers Credit Association, 375 Jackson Avenue, St. Louis, Missouri 63130, which contains within its weekly pages much information about regulations pertaining to credit and finance. The FTC issues a free weekly newsletter that headlines its weekly major activities. Trade associations, such as the Direct Mail/Marketing Association and the Direct Selling Association, send newsletters to members who are concerned with the regulations and laws that affect the mail-order and the door-to-door selling businesses. One could go on and on, but, as a first step, an informed seller should personally determine the best publications concerning her or his business, subscribe to them, and most important, read them.

chapter 4

The VIPs—organizations that act on behalf of the consumer

Every company, even the most diligent in serving and responding to its customers, can expect an occasional complaint from a VIP. All communications from such individuals or organizations should receive priority treatment. This, of course, means that the staff handling customer communications must be made aware of the existence and function of VIPs.

ORGANIZATIONS MERITING PRIORITY

To inform those persons in your company who are unfamiliar with the organizations that rate priority handling, the following discussions offer a summary of the nature and extent of many of them.

The expanding Federal Trade Commission

The Federal Trade Commission was set up in 1914 primarily to enforce antitrust legislation. Over the years, it has taken on more of the nature of a consumer advocacy organization. Where the commission finds a strong pattern of violation of consumer rights it may propose new regulations, and these have the effect of law. Usually, before such regulations go into effect, the industry most directly affected by the proposed new rules of doing business has a chance to present its case before the FTC. Various consumer advocates also are invited to speak on behalf of the consumer. And, of course, interested individuals can also speak out—if they somehow become aware that the hearings are scheduled. (The consumer advocates may become aware of upcoming hearings because one or more of the ten regional offices of the FTC publishes newsletters containing information of interest to the consumer.)

The so-called wrongdoings of the seller are not approached as crimes, and consequently the procedures of the FTC, used to enforce its mandate, are not the same as those usually associated with law enforcement. There is a marked absence of the procedural safeguards that surround both civil and criminal acts in the courts. The point must be made that as far as the seller is concerned, the power of the FTC is awesome.

FTC's basic operations. The FTC deals with consumer affairs in two basic ways:

1. *Guidelines and trade regulations.* From time to time the FTC publishes industry-wide guidelines or trade regulations that codify desired practices as they apply to specific industries. The guides and regulations have varying legal strengths, but in general they have the force of administrative law. Concerned sellers should be aware of the various rules that affect their businesses.

2. *Proceedings against individual companies.* The FTC may proceed against companies that in the commission's judgment are in violation of either the commission's guides or

rules, or it may proceed against companies for any practice that in the judgment of the FTC is unfair to the consumer. Various methods are used by the FTC in actions against individual companies. These range from seeking an assurance of voluntary compliance to a sort of trial before one of the FTC's hearing examiners. (Notice of such a hearing usually is made the subject of a news release, which is distributed to and published by many newspapers. The resulting news items could be very damaging to a company's business reputation.)

Because of the FTC's power to regulate business, it is most important that companies reply with dispatch to all communications from this federal agency, and make special efforts to satisfy any customer who complains to a district FTC office.

The U.S. Postal Service

Even though the U.S. Postal Service (USPS) is operated as a public corporation, and ostensibly is no longer a branch of the federal government, its strong powers—dating back to 1872—to take action where mail fraud is suspected have not diminished. Therefore, all communications from the USPS and its Office of the Consumer Advocate relating to what the USPS calls "failure to render" should receive priority treatment.

Here are some examples of what the USPS means by failure to render: failure to deliver, failure to make a "guaranteed" refund, delivery of goods in very poor condition, and delivery of merchandise that fails to come close to advertised claims.

If a company fails to satisfy the USPS, the service could unleash its ultimate weapon: stoppage of all mail addressed to the company for an examination in the presence of a postal inspector and a representative of the company. Those letters containing orders for the item under proscription are returned to the sender with an explanation.

Becoming subject to such an extreme measure takes many months and repeated violations. Nevertheless, no company seeking to maintain continuity in the marketplace wants to come even close to risking such restrictions. The remedy is clear: Treat all communications from the USPS with great care and speed.

The Better Business Bureau

Each local branch of the Better Business Bureau is a separate entity supported by the businessmen in the region in which it operates. Nevertheless, its 140 branches do act in concert through the Council of Better Business Bureaus, Inc., in Washington. The separate branches cooperate with each other. For example, if a customer in California believes he or she has been wronged by a merchant in New York City, the local BBB will forward the complaint to the BBB of Metropolitan New York. Executives of that organization will attempt to contact the merchant in question, first by phone and then by letter, if there is no response by phone or if the merchant has no phone, which is often the case for fly-by-night suppliers operating through a post office box.

No longer is it possible for fraudulent operators to maintain anonymity behind a post office box number. The USPS now requires that the name, address, and phone number of the renter of the box be revealed to complaining customers.

Beside acting in concert with each other, branches of the BBB also cooperate closely with the FTC, USPS, and consumer-advocacy organizations. Where a local BBB has good reason to believe that a company is operating in a patently fraudulent manner, it will ask the USPS to stop mail addressed to that company for examination in the manner previously described.

The BBB also has been promoting an arbitration procedure by which a consumer can obtain redress without the cost and delay associated with legal procedures. The arbitration procedure was first developed in 1970 by the BBB of Metropolitan New York, which is by far the largest bureau (it has satellite operations in Newark, New Jersey; in Harlem; in suburban Long Island, outside New York City; one for Bergen and Passaic counties, in northern New Jersey, and for Rockland county, just over the border in New York; and in Westchester, Putnam, and Dutchess counties in New York). Under this procedure, a company agrees to submit complaints from customers to binding arbitration. To make consumers aware that such arbitration is available, the companies subscribing to the procedure (they do not necessarily have to be supporters of their local BBB) are encouraged to enlighten customers on the availability of arbitration. From their local BBB (over 90 local BBBs now promote arbitration) they obtain decals, as illustrated in Figure 3. These decals should be prominently displayed, such as on entrance doors.

In addition, the following statement can be printed on sales receipts, tickets, and other documents received by the customer:

This firm has filed with The Better Business Bureau of (locality) a precommitment to be willing to arbitrate any controversy or claim arising out of this transaction in accordance with the Arbitration Rules of the Consumer-Business Arbitration Tribunal of The Better Business Bureau of (locality). To you the customer, this means that you can ask the Bureau to arbitrate any difference between us. We have already agreed to this procedure.

32

FIGURE 3

We participate in Arbitration for Business
and Customers through the
BETTER BUSINESS BUREAU

Decal provided by the Better Business Bureau for retailers participating in the organizaton's arbitration program.

Over 2,000 merchants in the New York Metropolitan area have subscribed to this arbitration procedure, and 13,000 nationally. To date, the number of "cases" settled by the arbitration procedure can only be counted in the hundreds each year. However, the number of customers taking advantage of the procedure should increase as a result of new legislation. On January 4, 1975, President Gerald Ford signed the new Consumer Product Warranty Law, which promotes such informal settlement of disputes. Most of the bureaus do not charge for arbitration, but some do charge a small fee from both customer and supplier.

To obtain more information on the arbitration procedure,

contact your local BBB. If there is no BBB in your locality, or if your BBB is one of the declining number that does not promote arbitration, information on the procedure can be obtained from the Better Business Bureau of Metropolitan New York, Inc., 110 Fifth Avenue, New York, New York 10011.

Even though the number of cases submitted for arbitration will most likely continue to remain small, especially in comparison with the huge number of transactions, the significance of arbitration is great. What the promotion of commitment to arbitration on the part of businesses does is to reinforce the confidence of the consumer in trading with participating companies. And increasing consumer confidence is what this book is all about.

Attorneys general and other governmental consumer advocates

It is becoming more and more the rule for state, municipal, and even county governments to appoint official consumer advocates. In this, they are as usual following the lead of the largest states, New York and California. As a resident of New York City, the author is most familiar with the strong pro-consumer stand taken by this state's attorney general, and by the city's commissioner of consumer affairs, who was formerly that activist ex–Miss America, Bess Myerson. The current commissioner, Elinor Guggenheimer, has her own weekly half-hour television show, "Consumer Game."

Neither the attorney general, currently that hustling septuagenarian, Louis Lefkowitz, nor the city's successive commissioners of consumer affairs hesitate to blast in the press what they consider to be negligent companies or industries. Local newspapers do indeed give these highly political advocates plenty of coverage. Even though any companies condemned by the consumer advocates usually are given an opportunity to rebut (as part of the same denunciatory article, or one appearing the following day) it is obvious that the thunderbolts hurled by the public advocates can do great damage. For example, one New York City retailer condemned by a consumer advocate was JGE Enterprises, a chain of discount franchises that had expanded rapidly under the impetus of the president's locally famous TV commercials, "What's the story, Jerry?" Even though this firm, through its well-known spokesman, rigorously defended its record, much damage had been done.

Again, the policy to be set by any company for the handling of correspondence from governmental consumer advocates is obvious: Priority treatment should be the unvarying rule. Don't try to counterpunch after a stinging denunciation in the press, which is always picked up by the local radio and TV stations. In this situation, an offense is never the best defense.

"Action Lines" popular in broadcasting

Consumer advocacy is "in," and local newspapers and magazines and radio and television stations already are on the bandwagon. No merchant or company that is condemned in print or on the air waves can blunt the denunciation by a rebuttal, no matter how well documented. The best defense is to avoid the denunciation.

One way to avoid being surprised by completely unanticipated denunciations is to maintain good relations with the press, including the news departments of local radio and TV stations. The fact that a company advertises in these media is no protection against denunciations. The company that maintains an open door policy for inquiries from the press is much more likely to be given an opportunity to blunt or at least rebut a denunciation. On the other hand, companies that antagonize the press with a rigid "no-comment" policy are not likely to be given a chance to protect their reputations. Reporters who are frustrated in their dealings with a company are much more likely to crucify that company when given the opening.

DMMA and its "Action Line"

Another organization that maintains an active "Action Line" is the Direct Mail/Marketing Association, 9 East 43d Street, New York, New York 10017.

DMMA's "Mail Order Action Line" is open to customers of any mail-order merchandiser, not just the 1,700 members of this association. DMMA reports that 80 percent of the complaints received for "Mail Order Action Line" are quickly resolved in favor of the customer.

Like the BBB, DMMA maintains close liaison with the FTC and the USPS, and also with the various BBB operations.

Trade associations

DMMA is not the only trade association that is trying to help the consumer with complaints against members of its association or those in the same industry. The Direct Selling Association (DSA), 1730 M Street, N.W., Washington, D.C. 20036, which is comprised of companies that sell door-to-door and by party plans, also responds to and follows up the consumer complaints it receives. Other associations of organizations that deal with the public already emulate the DMMA, or are planning to, by offering an avenue of complaint for the consumer. Because most companies want to maintain the respect of their competitors, it makes sense to give priority treatment to complaints forwarded through the DMMA, the DSA, and the other trade associations.

Attorneys representing the individual customer

Not aware of the various consumer advocates who will in effect represent them gratis against the merchant or manufacturer, a small percentage of unhappy customers can be expected to turn the matter over to an attorney. Since the amounts involved are often under $100, it is obvious that any capable and active attorney representing a client for such matters is writing to the merchant or manufacturer more as an accommodation to her or his client than on a fee basis. The client is either a businessman whose firm provides the lawyer with a lot of other revenue, or the lawyer is a close friend or relative of the aggrieved consumer and dispatches the letter as a favor.

Nevertheless, all such communications should be given priority treatment with an individually typed answer rather than a reply via form letter.

When the courts intervene

No businessman needs to be told that a summons from a court requires priority treatment. Now that Small Claims Courts are becoming the norm in most states and municipalities, many consumers without access to a lawyer may take their complaint to a small claims court. (What is defined as a "small claim" can be surprisingly substantial: in New York State the Small Claims Courts are now permitted to adjudicate claims of up to

$1,000.) Since many Small Claims Courts function at night, it makes sense to resolve such complaints before an appearance is required before a "testy" judge. (In the author's experience, the judges assigned to Small Claims Courts resent the night duty.)

Important distributors and dealers

Rarely will distributors and dealers take up the cudgels for their customers. Since the relationship with a productive dealer or distributor is more important to the company than the dollars represented by any one sale, such communications should of course be given special treatment. If many such letters of complaint are received by the company, it should consider setting up some means of redress at the dealer level, such as "over-the-counter" trade-ins of defective merchandise within some stated period, most commonly 90 days, but sometimes extending to six months and more.

THE SIGNIFICANCE OF "CONSUMERISM"

What is the significance of consumerism and the activities of all the consumer advocates? If you take the attitude that they are an unwarranted and unnecessary interference in your business, you will be bringing an aggravation upon yourself to no purpose (and your recalcitrance may communicate itself to those of your employees who are responsible for dealing with the consumer advocates).

"If you can't beat 'em, join 'em" is the smart posture, for two good reasons. First, by cooperating with the consumer advocates you will help reinforce consumer confidence in the businesses with which they deal, as well as in the free-enterprise system in general. Second, your company may gain an advantage over competitors who choose not to cooperate with the consumer advocates (except, of course, with the governmental agencies that can force compliance). The consumer advocates are not radicals dedicated to the destruction of American business. In fact, they have even handed out kudos to businesses that cooperate with them.

One watchdog group is named Public Action Coalition on Toys, which goes by the acronym of PACT, not to be confused with another New York-based group using the same acronym but standing for Provide Addict Care Today. The PACT of interest here is made up of no less than 18 organizations, the best known of which is the National Organization for Women (NOW). PACT is located at 38 West 9th Street, New York, New York 10011. In the past, PACT has picketed the American Toy Fair, a trade show held yearly in New York, to protest against toys considered dangerous, a stimulant to violence, sexist, or racist.

The first time that anyone protested publicly against "war" toys was during the first toy show after the assassination of President John F. Kennedy. There had been strong intimations that some mothers might protest against war toys. A leading manufacturer of such toys assigned an aide to investigate the charge that so-called war toys and play guns stimulated children, particularly little boys, to violence. The aide interviewed some leading child psychiatrists, who were of the opinion that the toys, far from stimulating violence, helped dissipate it. At first the president of the toy company planned to issue a news release to this effect, but cancelled dissemination of the release when it appeared that the mothers would not protest. But when the toy show opened a few days later, a group of mothers began picketing the building in which the show was taking place. They carried signs denouncing war toys and were well covered by the press. By then it was too late to issue the press release.

However, PACT, which was organized by members of Ralph Nader's staff, has now switched from picketing to prizes. Ten manufacturers were publicly congratulated for creating toys or books that won the admiration of PACT's members. The Quaker Oats Company was given a special citation for the "constructive policies" of two of its subsidiaries, Louis Marx Toys, which eliminated guns from its product lines, and Fisher-Price Toys, which advertises its products to adults instead of to children. The press conference at which the awards were presented was given excellent coverage in the *New York Times* of February 19, 1975. (In spite of PACT's efforts, there has been somewhat of a revival in "war" toys since the end of the Vietnam War.)

Now a framed award from some of Nader's Raiders is no substitute for black ink on the balance sheet—but the shift of consumer advocates from negative to positive approaches is to be welcomed by businessmen.

The future of consumerism

PACT illustrates two important trends in consumerism: coalitions of consumer advocates, and concentration on one industry of special interest. PACT is not the only coalition. Of far greater significance is the Consumer Federation of America, a fast-growing coalition of over 200 consumer organizations, labor unions, and rural-electric cooperatives. CFA, which is based in Washington, D.C.—at 1012 14th Street, N.W. 20005, (202) 737-3732—is headed by a dynamic woman, Carol

Tucker Foreman, who has no trouble gaining an audience on Capitol Hill. She and her supporters are pushing hard for an independent agency to represent the consumer before federal agencies and the courts. In 1974, the creation of this agency was blocked when its supporters failed by one vote to override a filibuster in the Senate.

Concentrating on a single industry is another consumerist approach that is gaining in effectiveness. There really is nothing new about concentrating on a single industry—Ralph Nader got his start by attacking the auto industry. Other industries under consumerist attack are petroleum, power, and telephone. Some states also have appointed officials who have expanded their roles from regulating certain industries to acting as ombudsmen for the customers of those industries. The best-known example is Herbert Denenberg, former head of the insurance commission of Pennsylvania. When he was commissioner, Denenberg issued pamphlets explaining to consumers how to avoid unnecessary surgical operations, quite an extension of his regulatory powers over insurers of health.

If yours is an industry that is focused on by the increasingly numerous and vocal consumer advocates, expect a flood of complaints from your customers. Answering these complaints isn't enough: You must also act, together with other members of your industry, through your trade association.

RECOMMENDED REFERENCE

Consumer Sourcebook, edited by Paul Wasserman and Jean Morgan, and published in 1974 by Gale Research Company (535 pages, $35), provides a directory and guide to the government agencies, the associations, and the consumer organizations where the consumer can go for satisfaction when a purchase proves faulty.

chapter 5

How to reduce customer communications

Although an efficient and effective customer service operation is not only essential and fully justified—in terms of the contribution it can and should make to company growth and success—nevertheless, it does represent overhead. The lower the volume of communications handled, the less the cost.

Minimizing unnecessary customer communications depends to some extent on how the customer service operation functions, but much more depends on the functioning of other parts of the business. Specifically, marketing, distribution, packaging, and billing.

HOW MARKETING CAN REDUCE UNNECESSARY COMMUNICATIONS

The marketing department can reduce unnecessary communications in several ways. First, by making sure the customer understands just what he or she is being offered. The "deal" should not be vague nor worded in terms that lead the customer to think he's getting something other than what's actually de-

41

livered. Explain clearly the customer's obligations and the "return" and "refund" privileges, if any. True, he may keep something that disappoints him and never communicate his dissatisfaction with the purchase, but will he ever buy anything from that supplier again?

Prepare legible catalogs

Catalogs and other promotions should be designed in an easy-to-follow manner with clear, legible type, not only to avoid unnecessary communications but mainly to stimulate sales. One of the big mistakes made in many catalogs is having type so small that it requires a magnifying glass to read it.

This matter of tiny print brings to mind the story told by Leo Lionni, the distinguished art director. Very early in his career he was employed by an advertising agency that included among its accounts a manufacturer of steam locomotives. Lionni laid out what he proudly considered an attractive full-page ad, but all the text type was six or eight point. The head of the agency was also very impressed with the "new look" of the ads and took Lionni along to meet the president of the locomotive company, who reviewed all ads prior to release. The president praised Lionni's work, but then told him to change all the type to ten point. As he put it, "By the time a customer has risen to the point where he approves the purchase of a new $200,000 locomotive, he is approaching 65 and wears bifocals."

So whenever you begin work on a new catalog, remind the designer of all those sixtyish customers with bifocals.

Not only is the type size of importance, so is the way in which the price is placed in relation to the catalog number. When the price is on the same line as the catalog number, problems are avoided. On the other hand, where the catalog designer is trying too hard to jam too much information on a page, and places the price on another line, some customers are confused. They either can't find the price, or they pick up some other price. The result is inaccuracies on the order form, with unnecessary communication between the company and customer to clear up the discrepancies.

Problems frequently arise, too, in relating the catalog picture, the copy (description), and the catalog number. Be sure the picture is clearly keyed to the copy and that the key identification is prominently located, in large type and on a light background. This will prevent the customer from visualizing one item and ordering another.

Avoid illegible colors. For ease of reading and highest legibility, stick to black print on white paper. Recently, one well-known mail-order specialist, in apparently attempting to capitalize on the current nostalgia trend, printed its catalog of "old-fashioned" (but newly manufactured) merchandise on brownish paper. The small type in the catalog was very hard to read. Also avoid printing type in yellow, orange, or red on white; it's hard to read. However, dark blue on white is nearly as legible as black.

Include more than one order form. Mail-order catalogs should contain more than one order form. Two are recommended, plus the enclosure of additional forms in the customer's shipment. However, each supplier must determine for himself just how many forms are required. In a few rare instances, where the customer or members of his or her family keep on using the catalog all year round, three or even four order forms may make sense. Part of the trade-off is between the added cost of printing and binding the additional order forms and the extra cost and disruption of processing orders that arrive in nonstandard format. Your clerks may encounter difficulties in deciphering orders written on blank sheets of paper.

For example, one mail-order firm once received an order from a good customer on her personal stationery. The 14 items were numbered by the customer from one to 14. Shortly after the order was shipped, the traffic manager received a frantic call from the driver of the delivery truck. The customer had refused to accept her shipment, which nearly filled his truck.

What went wrong? The unthinking order clerk had entered one of item one, two of item two, and so forth, down to 14 matched sets of luggage!

If you don't bind in enough order forms, list all the information that must be provided as a guide to the customer who has used up the forms included in the catalog. And if many of your customers do not speak English as a first language, include these instructions in other languages—see under "Special Situations" on p. 56.

Where clothing and shoes are involved, provide careful instructions on how to measure body dimensions for proper sizing; don't depend on the customer's recollection of his or her size. Since the last time they purchased a similar item they may have put on weight—or they sometimes delude themselves into ordering a smaller size than they actually require.

For excellent examples, see the instructions on sizing in the yellow pages in the Penney's, Sears', and Ward's general catalogs. The clever approach taken by the Haband Company is interesting. It includes a paper tape measure 50 inches long folded in with many of the direct-mail offerings.

HOW EFFICIENT DISTRIBUTION
CAN REDUCE COMMUNICATIONS

The customer can be disappointed in several ways. Aside from poor product performance, he may be stimulated to complain about the slow delivery of what is ordered. In my experience, the customer does not expect that an item ordered by mail or phone will be delivered the next day, but he will become restive when more than three weeks pass without delivery. If the merchant advertises "fast delivery" but fails to deliver within two weeks, expect inquiries. Therefore, no company should advertise "24-hour service" or "immediate delivery" if it actually does not ship for several weeks.

There's a much more important reason why speed of delivery should be emphasized: to make the order stick, since many items are ordered on impulse. If it takes weeks for the item to be delivered, it may no longer be of interest. There's also the risk that with delayed delivery the customer may purchase a substitute at retail.

In a test conducted by a direct marketing organization, the rate of returns was 20 percent less among shipments that arrived promptly, compared to those that arrived late.

The frequent complaints of slow delivery should decline sharply now that the Federal Trade Commission requires that the great majority of mail-order merchants fill their orders within 30 days (if no period is specified) or offer the customer a refund or credit. Cash refunds must be made within seven working days, and a credit executed within one billing cycle. Efficient organizations will have no trouble complying, while the inefficient or neglectful will have to toe the mark—or go out of business.

Incidentally, some companies acknowledge all orders with a postcard specifying approximate shipping date in order to curtail "where is my order?" inquiries. However, where order volume is high, this can be an expensive routine, and should be avoided unless you are absolutely unable to put your merchandise in the customer's hands within three weeks.

Importance of keeping items in stock

One sure way to generate an avalanche of unwanted and unnecessary customer correspondence is to fail to anticipate the extent of orders, then have to refuse, cancel, or create back orders.

No marketing chief can claim a very high percentage of correct prophecies of sales for new items. But it is surprising how close an experienced marketer can come to gauging demand for newly marketed products after initial orders have been received. Therefore, some mechanism should always be provided for measuring and quickly reporting the *first incoming* orders so that "hot" items can be spotted, additional stock ordered, and their delivery expedited.

During the period of intense shortages experienced in 1974, it was almost impossible for many companies to match deliveries to orders. If such an unusual situation arises again (and it is highly likely), companies must be prepared to tighten their inventory controls to make sure that goods under promotion will be available to match predictions of sales. Also, market intelligence and production statistics must be obtained and scrutinized to forecast impending shortages, so that goods not likely to be available are not promoted.

Then there are the companies that are unable to fill many orders because of employee pilferage or collusion between warehouse employees and truckmen, all of which results in unexpected inventory shortages. Finally, there are companies whose records are so sloppy they don't know what is on hand, and keep on accepting orders for goods no longer in stock.

Detailed analyses of operating conditions causing customer correspondence almost always place merchandise shortages as the number one problem. When a company is out of stock on too many items and this is creating extensive back orders, the additional cost of handling a large volume of customer inquiries and complaints must be expected. This can be avoided with proper inventory controls and forecasting techniques.

Understandable manuals for installation, operation, and repair

One sure way to generate many unneeded letters and phone calls from customers is to provide inadequate guidance on the installation, operation, and repair of complex products. This is one aspect of marketing in which all too many companies fall down. After manufacturing an excellent product and distributing it at an attractive price, they thoughtlessly skimp on the installation, operation, and repair manuals. When the manuals are inadequate, the problem can most commonly be traced to poor or insufficient illustrations. However, some manuals simply fail to provide the proper instructions. In other words, *it is impossible* to install, operate, or adjust the product according to the enclosed instructions.[1]

"How could this be?" one might ask. The explanation is very simple: the instructions are faulty because they are hur-

---

[1] For guidance in preparing manuals, I suggest that you request a copy of a 38-page booklet, *Technical Publications Guidelines,* from the National Association of Service Managers, 6650 Northwest Highway, Chicago, Illinois 60631. The price is $2.

riedly updated versions of manuals for superseded products. Instead of ordering new manuals at the time the new models go into production, some executive neglects this important chore till the last minute.

Another common reason for inadequate manuals is that they are translated from another language. With so many electronic and photographic products of oriental manufacture, it is not surprising that too many of the manuals appear to be translations of brochures written originally in Japanese or Chinese. Unfortunately, the translators often are not familiar with English and produce manuals that are not only difficult to read but often ungrammatical and full of misspellings and typographical errors. Such manuals, which represent at most 1 or 2 percent of the cost of bringing the product to the customer, can do nothing but lower confidence in the product and its supplier. If you arrange for manufacture of a product overseas, or import a complex product from overseas, make sure that a well-illustrated, complete brochure in idiomatic English is prepared in this country by experts in the creation of manuals. (The printing could be done abroad, but insist that sturdy paper stock is selected, not some pulp grade that quickly yellows or even disintegrates.) If you need any models, take those produced by leading U.S. manufacturers, such as Kodak and RCA.

Here is another area to be explored with regard to these essential manuals: Is there some way they can be inserted in or attached to the product, the way an owner's manual should be kept in the glove compartment of a car? Manufacturers should add little slots or pigeonholes to their products so that applicable manuals can be kept there and not misplaced or lost, which is so often the case.

To accommodate the many good customers who will lose or

deface (by spilling coffee on?) their instruction manuals, always print an adequate overstock and store them convenient to the customer service department. One of the functions of this department is to replace such manuals, which should logically be right at hand—and already inside shipping envelopes.

Providing local service. No matter how well a company prepares its operation and repair manuals, some products will in time require the services of a professional. One sure way to generate a lot of complaints from irate customers is failure to instruct those who service your products in the intricacies of new models. Some companies do a superb job of making sure that local service personnel understand a new model *before* it reaches the hands of customers. Others wait until the flow of customer complaints reaches flood stage to take barely adequate measures.

The easy-to-follow order form

All of us have been filling out forms since we were teenagers: applications for schools, licenses, jobs, and the like. In view of the familiarity of every person in business with forms, and the wide availability of good models, it's amazing to encounter so many poorly designed forms. The inadequate forms under scrutiny here are order forms.

To help the customer provide accurate, needed information, and to encourage legible writing, here are some specific recommendations concerning order forms. (Samples of recommended forms are shown in Figures 4, 5, and 6.)

How to create good order forms. Provide sufficient space between lines so the customer can write his name and address without being forced to scribble in a cramped and pos-

FIGURE 4

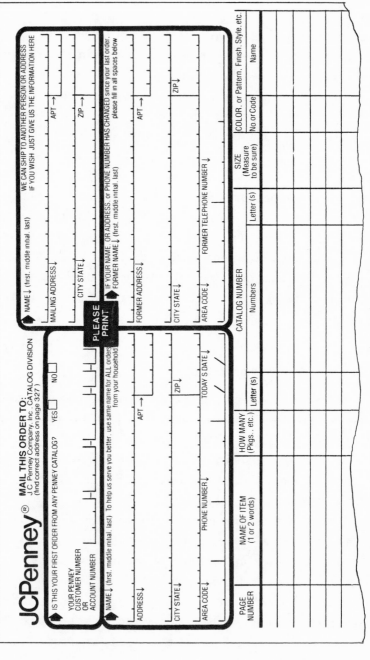

Order form provided in the J. C. Penney catalog, with tick marks to encourage the customer to print.

FIGURE 5

W. ATLEE BURPEE CO.

See the famous Burpee Guarantee
on Reverse Side

300 Park Avenue
Warminster, Pa. 18991

656 40

(1) For faster and more accurate service, please attach peel-off label from back cover here.

Place Label Here

(2) Please print all information below if label is not available or is incorrect. Use same name (First, Initials, Last) for all orders from your household.

Name _____ Date _____

Street/Hwy. and No. _____

R. R. No. _____ Box No. _____

City _____ State _____ Zip _____

Please use separate sheet for writing all inquiries or comments.

Phone _____

☐ Please send additional information on the Burpee English Greenhouse.

(3) Special instructions for seeds: Enter in "Pkg. Size Code" column the boxed letter (for Example [A]) preceding the Pkg. Size. Enter in "How Many" column the number of units you want.

	Catalog No.	Pkg. Size Code	How Many	Name of Item	Price	
1	—					
2	—					
3	—					
4	—					
5	—					
6	—					
7	—					
8	—					
9	—					
10	—					
11	—					
12	—					
13	—					
14	—					
15	—					

Please continue your order on the other side.

(4) Total above

(5) Total from other side

Handling Charge — **50**

BURPEE PAYS POSTAGE
Everything offered in the Burpee Catalog will be delivered postpaid anywhere in the Continental U. S. at the prices quoted.

(6) Sub-Total

(7) Pa. Sales Tax: 6% (Except gloves and boots)
Florida Sales Tax: 4% (Except vegetable seeds)

PLEASE USE THIS CONVENIENT ORDER FORM

(8) Total Amount Enclosed

Order form showing step-by-step numbering to guide the customers in complete and accurate written preparation.

FIGURE 6

It's Easy to Order from BURPEE!

**You can help us give you better service…
by ORDERING EARLY…avoid the last minute rush…
BE SURE YOUR ORDER FORM IS PROPERLY COMPLETED**

Five Digit
Catalog Number

Package Size
Code

How Many

Correct Address

Pre Addressed Label

W. Atlee Burpee Co.
Warminster, Pa. 18974

See the famous Burpee Guarantee
on Reverse Side

MR JOHN J JONES
234 YOUR STREET
ANYTOWN   PA 18966

(2) Please print all information below if label is not available or is incorrect Use same name (First, Initials, Last) for all orders from your household

Name *Mr. John J. Jones*

Street/Hwy and No *679 Main Street*

R. R. No   Box No

Please use separate sheet for writing all inquiries or comments

City *Anytown*   State *Pa.*   Zip *18966*

(3) Special instructions for seeds. Enter in "Code" column the boxed letter (for Example Ⓐ) preceding the Pkg. Size. Enter in "How Many" column the number of units you want.

	Catalog No	Code	How Many	Name of Item	Price	
1	*1410-0*	*C*	*1*	*Dwarf Fruit Tree Orchard*	*26*	*95*
2	*7866-7*	*C*	*1*	*Bicentennial Hyacinth Coll.*	*9*	*25*
3	*7400-5*		*25*	*Elizabeth Arden Tulips*	*6*	*25*
4	*5351-2*	*A*	*2*	*Pixie Hybrid Tomato*	*1*	*40*
5	*1553-7*		*1*	*Snowcloud Flowering Crab*	*12*	*35*
6	*9252-8*		*1*	*Long Handled Bulb Planter*	*5*	*50*

1 Use the pre addressed label from the back cover of your catalog It's easy to peel off and affix to the order form where indicated

2 Use the pre addressed label even if it is incorrect or if you have moved. Print or type the correct name and address in the space provided If this is your second order, print or type your name and address (Use the same name for all orders from your household Example John J Jones)

3 Use the five digit catalog number here You will find this number directly at the beginning or end of the description paragraphs for all items offered in the catalog

4 The package size codes are located at the end of the description paragraphs on the same line as the prices and are alphabetic letters in boxes Example Ⓐ Be sure you enter a size code on **all** seed orders You will not have size codes for bulbs. nursery and merchandise items

5 How many should tell us how many of that particular size you are ordering If you are ordering collections. specials or sets. please enter the letter code Ⓒ in the "Code" Column and the number of collections desired in the "How Many" Column. **not** the number of items in the collections The letter code Ⓒ and the catalog number automatically indicate that this is a collection and how many items are in it

If you live in Pennsylvania. Florida. Illinois. Iowa or California. you may be required to pay sales tax Please check the instructions on the reverse side of the order form for details

Double check the addition on your order so that you will remit the correct amount of money. The best way to send money is money order. bank draft or check Please do not send postage stamps. coins or paper money

If we are sold out of the variety ordered. we will select one horticulturally similar or superior. and of equal or greater value If our selections are not acceptable. we will promptly refund your money

**HELP US FILL YOUR ORDER
QUICKLY AND ACCURATELY**

Please be especially careful when ordering items offered in sets—bulb collections. tool sets. fruit tree and berry collections Enter the letter code Ⓒ in the "Code" Column and the number of collections desired in the "How Many" Column. **not** the number of items in the collection The letter codeⒸ and the catalog number automatically tell us that this is a collection and how many items are in it

Easy-to-follow instructions on how to complete an order form.

sibly illegible manner. To make sure that the all-important name and address are legible, more and more mail-order houses are printing the catalog address labels for their regular customers in peel-off, self-adhesing form so they can be transferred from the cover of the catalog and pasted on the order form where indicated. (See Figure 5.) Of course, this only applies to the initial order generated by the catalog. However, that covers a substantial percentage of orders received. (Inquiries at mail-order houses using this technique indicate that from 70 to 80 percent of all order forms arrive with the transferable labels, which makes the practice economically viable. The added cost of a removable label versus the conventional nonremovable label is on the order of $2.40 per thousand.) Of course, this type of label should be used for former customers only (not prospects), where the extra cost can be clearly justified.

To also ensure legibility of name and address, many order forms are printed with tick marks or squares in the places where name and address are written. This tends to just about force the customer to block print. (See Figure 4.)

Because the abbreviations for some of the states are so similar, particularly if the customer follows the two-letter abbreviations concocted by the Postal Service (MA for Massachusetts, ME for Maine, and MO for Missouri), some companies (one example is F.A.O. Schwarz, the famous New York-based toy retailer) ask that customers write out the complete name of the state. This may not be necessary if enough space is left for writing in a clear abbreviation. Besides, in today's mechanized post offices the zip code is the overriding criterion. So be sure and leave plenty of room for the zip code, and emphasize that the customer include it.

Why apartment and phone numbers are often needed.
As part of the address, the order form should ask for the customer's apartment number, which may not be listed on the directory of the building. Thus, if the item can't be delivered by the postman or the United Parcel Service because no one is home, the postman or truckman will be able to leave a note that an attempt has been made to deliver. If the package was shipped parcel post, the customer can then go to the local post office and pick up his purchase. (Another reason so many merchants favor UPS over Parcel Post is that the former makes three attempts to deliver, compared to just one for the latter.)

The customer's phone number should be requested, too, just in case the order form can't be understood, is illegible, needed information is missing or there is a good chance the customer will not accept the substitution made by those who check incoming orders. Particularly where the order involves expensive merchandise, it's well worth calling the customer long-distance to clarify the order or to request permission for a substitution. The customer is not only grateful, but also quite favorably impressed.

Step-by-step numbering. Most order forms require a number of steps for completion. To guide the customer through the intricacies of an order form, step-by-step numbers should be included, as shown in (see Figure 5) the simple but effective order form of the W. Atlee Burpee Company, the seed company celebrating its 100 years in business in 1976. Printing the guide numbers in reverse blocks or even in color encourages accurate completion of the form.

Ordering instructions, particularly those that anticipate questions that might arise, are greatly appreciated and used by customers. Like the step-by-step numbering, they act as a checklist and insure that all of the needed information is being provided. It has always amazed me how many companies fail to include written instructions on how to order. Mail-order businesses where 75 to 85 percent of their year's sales is received in six weeks—such as Christmas gift sellers and mail-order seed and nurserymen—do an excellent job of supplying instructions (see Figures 6 and 7). They have found that there's practically no

FIGURE 7

The Swiss Colony

HOW TO ORDER

1. Print or type all names and addresses to avoid errors.
2. Indicate ZIP CODE in your address. The Post Office will assist with your GIFTEE zip codes.
3. All items are available for shipment September 1 through May 31, unless otherwise indicated.
4. Greetings are automatically shown on each gift shipment. Personal greeting cards are not necessary.
5. Please keep a copy of your order for personal reference.
6. Write additional names on your own stationery and attach, if necessary.

COMPLETE ALL ORDERS

Please be sure your giftee addresses are correct, complete and current. If you are not sure of an address at the present time, send that part of your order later, when you have the exact address.

CHANGES IN YOUR ORDER

Changes in Christmas delivery instructions or gift selections must reach us prior to Nov. 27th. We are unable to make changes after that date.

DELIVERY TIME REQUIRED

Please send your Christmas order early. It should reach us before December 10 for assurance that your gift will arrive in time. If we feel unsure about timely arrival, we write your giftee that your gift is coming.

WEIGHTS

Shipping weights stated in our brochure refer to weight classifications on the Post Office rate chart.

SUBSTITUTIONS

We reserve the right to substitute items of equal value in a gift if necessary (especially for orders received after Dec. 10). Even so, you must be pleased as each gift is guaranteed.

PAYMENT

Please make checks or money orders payable to The Swiss Colony or use your credit card. Do not send currency or stamps. Sorry no C.O.D.

PRICES

GIFT ASSORTMENTS — Pages 2-57 are quoted postpaid. No delivery charge need be added for shipments to any address in the U.S. (All 50 states).

OVERSEAS SHIPMENTS

Sorry, we cannot ship meat, flowers, fruit or plants.
Overseas shipments are available ONLY to Hawaii, Alaska, U.S. Possessions, Canada, APO & FPO addresses AT THE BUYERS RISK. Sorry, our guarantee does *not* apply.
APO & FPO— Christmas order deadline November 15. MUST be zip coded. To insure air service, all are sent via P.A.L. (Parcel Air Lift). Add $1.00 for this service.
U.S. POSSESSIONS— Christmas order deadline November 21. Add $1.00 for postage and handling.
CANADA — Christmas order deadline November 21. Please furnish Canadian Zip Code. Add $2.00 for postage and handling.
ALASKA & HAWAII— Christmas order deadline November 21. No additional Postage required.

WE VALUE YOUR ORDER

We can assure you we give each order personal attention. If you are not completely satisfied with the way your order was handled, please notify our Customer Service Department giving your order number. Every effort will be made to correct or explain the situation to your satisfaction.

GUARANTEE

We are proud of the reputation earned during our 50 years as the leading mail order food gift house, a reputation for reliability, integrity, with gifts of superlative quality. Every item is guaranteed to be exactly as advertised — and delivered in perfect condition anywhere in the U.S proper, provided we were given the correct address.

Clear information about the ordering and the shipments is given in the order form of the Swiss Colony, food purveyors, of Monroe, Wisconsin.

time to write the customer for missing information if delivery is to be made before Christmas or planting time, hence the order must be complete and correct when it is first received.

Contingency delivery instructions. To further insure that customers receive items ordered on time some merchants, such as B. Altman & Co., New York, include in their order form a line titled "Delivery Instructions." The apartment-dweller customer can include such useful information as, "If not home, leave with super." The customer who resides in a private home can insert, "If not home, leave with neighbor at No. 39." The United Parcel Service will follow such instructions if they are part of the shipping label.

Special situations

Some businesses by their very nature call for special measures to cut down on unnecessary correspondence from customers.

One of these is the insurance industry, which is required by law or practice to use legal terminology in its policies. This terminology confuses most people, resulting in a heavy volume of queries. Since it could not change the language of its policies, one insurance carrier came up with a simple and effective way to cut down on what was essentially unproductive correspondence—for both parties. A short folder was created that explained in simple English many of the terms that were causing the most queries. This folder is now inserted with all policies and has been very effective in cutting down on queries seeking explanations of what's in the policy.

Special instructions for the non-English speaking person. Companies that deal with many customers whose first language is not English should consider including ordering instructions or other required information in those languages. Decades ago, the major catalog houses routinely included ordering instructions in German and Swedish for the benefit of the many immigrants among their customers. The 1922 Ward's catalog contained ordering instructions in Czechoslovakian, German, Spanish, French, Dutch, Italian, Norwegian, Polish, Portuguese, Russian, Finnish, and Swedish.

Avoid indiscriminate substitutions

"Logical" substitutions can often be made where the substitute is quite close in color or function to the item ordered. However, indiscriminate or inadequate substitutions must be avoided. They will generate not only a lot of communications but costly cancellations as well.

This is what happened to one of the major petroleum companies that followed the now-common practice of including an offer of merchandise with its monthly charge account bills. The item in question was a hand calculator. When far more orders were received than anticipated, the organization handling the offer shipped a different and slightly less expensive calculator to many customers. Enough customers objected to the substitution to force the company to recall all the substitutes at great expense.

If all the parts of a set of goods are not available, don't ship the goods. For example, if a woman orders a pants suit, don't ship the pants without the top, or vice versa. If sent separately, the top and pants could come from different dye lots and might not match in color. If a fishing rod and reel set are ordered, both must be shipped together. Obviously, neither can be used alone.

HOW PROPER PACKAGING CAN REDUCE UNNECESSARY COMMUNICATIONS

Aside from the obvious role that packaging plays in getting the product to the customer in proper condition, those who package products can also help make sure that no unnecessary customer communications are generated. First of all, if the product is compact and of high value, such as a camera, watch, tape recorder, electric razor, or jewelry, the address label or carton should not carry any clues as to the contents. This includes the name of the manufacturer or distributor if that would be revealing. This is one sure way to cut down on the enormous amount of pilferage associated with the movement of goods on common carriers, including the U.S. Postal Service.

If the shipment is made in more than one carton, indicate clearly on each carton that it represents "Carton No. 1 of a two-carton shipment." If the product involves more than one part or has attachments, or if several items ordered by the customer are delivered in the same carton, that carton should contain a packing list. If for any reason some part, accessory, or ordered item is not included in the package, the packing slip should indicate which items are missing and what provisions have been made to get them to the customer, i.e., "being shipped under separate cover," "will be forwarded in two weeks," and so on.

Also, if a substitution has been made, this important fact should be brought to the customer's attention. Here's a suggested form to follow:

Unfortunately, the item you ordered is no longer available in blue (color). However, it is in stock in aquamarine (color), and we have taken the liberty of making this close substitution in color because we are aware that you are anxious to obtain this item. If you are not satisfied with the substitution, please return the contents to us in this carton for a complete refund or credit.

If the item requires a battery ("not supplied") for operation, or if it must be plugged into a power outlet to operate, this fact should be made quite clear. "Isn't this obvious?" you might ask. Well, it may be apparent to the people who are employed by the company that makes the item, but such requirements are not always apparent to the customer. This failure to communicate will result in many irate letters to manufacturers complaining that their products don't work. All too often, subsequent correspondence reveals that the naive customer did not realize that a battery was required, or that the power cord (perhaps retractable and concealed) should be plugged in.

If the product is complex enough to require putting it together, assembly and operational instructions must be included in the package. In fact, the booklet also should be listed on the packing slip to help make sure that the customer does not throw it out with the discarded packaging. All too often some key part, such as a nut or bolt, is thrown out with the packaging—stimulating unneeded correspondence. One way to avoid this is to follow the now common practice of bagging all small unattached parts in plastic. However, if the customer has thrown away some small, vital part, send him a replacement without charge.

Finally, the packing slip should contain instructions to the user on how to communicate with the company if she or he has any problems with the product enclosed. As indicated in Chapter 1, inclusion of such instructions will not result in any increase at all in customer communications. (See Figures 1 and 2 for an example of such a packing slip.) Incidentally, the use of a packing slip does as much as any other single element to speed and simplify customer service.

The nonreusable carton

Some manufacturers and distributors have chosen to ship their products in cartons and packages that can't be reused by the recipient to return the contents to the supplier if the customer is unhappy with them. It should be obvious that such devices to discourage customer returns are not appropriate, and should not be employed by any company seeking to generate additional business.

HOW THE BILLING DEPARTMENT CAN CUT UNNECESSARY COMPLAINTS

The billing department has a direct and simple role to play in cutting unneeded communications from customers. First of all, any bills should explain why the customer is charged a sales tax if the company maintains a facility in the same state from which the order originates (even if the items ordered are shipped from outside that state).

Customer confusion about sales taxes generates a great deal of communications, most of which could be avoided if the bill clearly stated why the sales tax is charged.

It should be obvious that no bill should arrive before the

merchandise charged for in the document. This is another source of irritation and unneeded communications. Time your billing so that bills arrive *immediately* after delivery. Better still, include the invoice in the package or affixed to the outside, as is commonly done by record and book clubs.

Use of diplomatic language in billing

An officer of one of the large Blue Cross agencies recently related an incident about a furious policyholder. This person called the president of the agency complaining about the unsympathetic letter she had just received, which opened with this sentence: "We are very happy to provide you with the final hospital bills of your late husband."

Mail all refund checks promptly. The customer may need the money to reorder from another company, and will write quickly if the check is not forthcoming a few days after notification. Refund to the penny on all transactions (some companies even refund the postage expended by the customer when unsatisfactory merchandise is returned).

If the order cannot be completely filled, both packing slip and bill should contain references to this fact, with proper adjustments on the bill, of course. Naturally, the customer should receive some indication when the missing items will be shipped, and also be given an opportunity to cancel the rest of the order if he or she so desires.

Finally, if the issue between the customer and merchant reaches the point where an unpaid bill is turned over to a collection agency, choose such an agency with great care. Some are not only highly abrasive, but even use illegal or at least highly questionable methods to obtain added information about the customer or to collect bills; for example, sending the customer a document on stationery that suggests it originated with a governmental agency. This may bring down the wrath of the consumer advocates, and much bad publicity.

HOW THE CUSTOMER RELATIONS DEPARTMENT CAN CUT COMPLAINTS

The customer relations department itself can eliminate many unneeded communications from customers by adopting rational policies. Here are several recommendations:

1. *Respond quickly.* A quick, informal response is much more satisfactory to the customer than a long-delayed formal communication.

2. *Use plain talk.* In both your form and personal letters avoid technical terms, jargon, and slang—and, of course, hackneyed phrases. Be modern, crisp, efficient. In short, be short (see Figure 8).

3. *Don't ask for proof of purchase.* Unless a substantial amount of money or merchandise is involved, accept the customer's word. Long experience indicates that the overwhelming majority of customers is honest. If they make a claim, it is correct in all but a small percentage of instances. (The money or merchandise "ripped off" each year in this manner by the rare con artists is most likely less than the cost of requesting proof of purchase from all other correspondents; so it's obviously not worth discomforting and antagonizing the honest customers by asking them to prove that they either paid for, never received, or returned merchandise.) The dollar limit on requesting copies of checks, insurance receipts, and the like can be set as high as $100, but usually ranges from $10 to $25.

FIGURE 8

Use plain talk

Avoid this kind of "businessese"

Dear Mr. Jones:

We are in receipt of your letter of November 11, and are pleased to inform you that the merchandise you requested is presently at hand and will be forwarded to you in accordance with the instructions you were so kind to specify in your previous letter of October 30.

It is a pleasure to be of service to you in this instance and we hope you will contact us if you have any further inquiries.

Use this direct approach:

Dear Mr. Jones:

Your order of November 3 will be shipped November 15 via United Parcel Service.

4. Acknowledge all returns and cancellations. A postcard acknowledgement is satisfactory.

5. Back orders. If you must back order, cancel them after 30 days and mail a refund unless the customer specifically requests you to hold the order. This has been the law in several states for years, and is now a national requirement as dictated by the FTC. Report to the customer via postcard (unless the item is of a highly personal nature), and report every three weeks the status of the back orders in force.

EXCESSIVE COMMUNICATIONS REFLECT A TROUBLED BUSINESS

It should be apparent after reading the preceding discussions that the level of communications from customers is an accurate reflection of the way a company conducts its business.

The company that receives a minimum number of complaints in relation to volume or number of transactions is in nearly all instances a healthy, growing business. Conversely, the company that is inundated with complaints from customers is obviously in trouble.

chapter 6

Staffing a customer communications function

Properly staffing a customer service function is a key element in its success. The process of staffing this function begins with the executive who has the responsibility for recruiting or designating the department head, who, typically, has the title of Customer (or Consumer) Relations (or Service) Manager; Director of Consumer Affairs; Consumer Advisor to the President; or Vice President, Consumer Action.

The executive with the responsibility for choosing the head of this department must be utterly convinced of the necessity of the department—and that it will make an important contribution to the success of the company. If, on the contrary, this executive sees the selection process as a chore to be sloughed off as quickly as possible with the least effort, then the person she or he has chosen will reflect this negligent attitude. There's a good chance the person will be some "dead wood" who has been chosen because the person is approaching retirement or has been superseded elsewhere.

THE "IDEAL" MANAGER OF
CUSTOMER RELATIONS

To help you and your company in selecting the man or woman to head the customer response function, here is a guide of the most important attributes:

1. *Knowledge of the organization.* The person chosen must, of course, be familiar with the products or services offered by the company and how orders are processed. The person should also be known to the managers of the various departments with which he or she will interact, such as marketing, manufacturing, finance, and distribution. Obviously, this may appear to preclude the hiring of an outsider for the job. However, if a company were forced to hire an outsider, because no suitable executive could be found within company ranks, this person should be given a period of weeks (and preferably at least a month) to become thoroughly familiar with the company and all its products. If the company has important branch operations, she or he should be permitted to visit the remote branches and get to know the personnel in charge.

2. *Good administrator.* Since customer service is a "people" operation (contrasted with a "mechanical" operation), in which healthy relations between its members is essential to success, the executive in charge must be a good administrator.

3. *Thorough and attentive to detail.* By its nature the customer service function deals with thousands of separate documents. The staff of the department must be thorough in its work, which means that the head of the department must set a good example. To insure thoroughness, careful but not too elaborate records must be kept of work flow. These records not only help insure that every single incoming communica-

tion gets attention, but also provide a means for measuring the productivity of the department.

4. *Articulate.* The head of the department must be able to communicate verbally with different groups: customers, dealers, other executives in the company, and on occasion, with consumer groups, consumer advocates, and VIPs.

5. *Informal.* Since informality is so important in achieving efficient customer relations, it should be obvious that the head of the department must be a person who relishes directness and informality. The same informality should extend to dealings with those inside the company. Often, a problem with a customer or dealer can be resolved by a short phone call to some other executive. If an executive finds it essential to have intracompany communications typed by a secretary (with many "for your information" copies to others), the person is not a good candidate for the head of customer service.

6. *Tolerant and even-tempered.* The department head must also be a person who by his or her nature has these two qualities. The person must be tough-skinned enough to shrug off the rare insult or the crotchety customer who can't be appeased.

7. *Enthusiastic.* The work of a customer response department is neither exciting nor varied. To maintain employee spirit and morale, it is essential that the head of this department exude enthusiasm. If he or she treats work as drudgery, this negative attitude will soon infect the staff.

If all of the above sounds as though it could only be embodied in some knight in shining armor, be assured that the many companies which have set up consumer affairs departments have been able to find the right men or women within their own organizations. One reason may be the challenge of the job—starting a new and useful function within the company.

Likely sources for this paragon

Companies should begin by looking into their public relations function, if they have one, for candidates. "Flacks," as they are referred to in the trade, are people whose business is to create a favorable image for the organization. They are diplomatic and very much people oriented. They also should be good at following up on details. Characteristically, they are usually quite articulate and adept at writing (or they couldn't handle public relations in the first place). Not too surprisingly, some top-notch department heads come out of public relations. Also, in some big corporations, like the J. C. Penney Company, the head of the "Educational and Consumer Relations Department" reports to the manager of public relations.

Most report to marketing. Some very competent managers have formerly been in sales. (And in the majority of companies, especially many large corporations, such as General Motors, the "Corporate Owner Relations Manager" reports to the vice president of marketing.) Sales personnel frequently bring a background of face-to-face contact with customers on problems relating to quality and service. Further, they have been well indoctrinated on the importance of "keeping customers and keeping them happy."

Less likely sources. In general, the finance or purchasing functions are not the best sources for candidates. Executives with such backgrounds, although good paper shufflers, tend to be too rigid, and are frequently suspicious that the customer is trying to take advantage of the company. Such is not at all the case. Experience has shown that most customers are fundamentally honest and only a tiny minority are out to bilk the seller.

Excellent sources of managers. Two ex-naval officers are doing very well indeed. They were hired directly after retiring. Operating in accordance with precise navy regulations and skill in handling people probably gave them excellent backgrounds.

Don't neglect women as candidates. One highly competent manager of consumer relations is an ex-supervisor of telephone operators. Executive secretaries and school teachers are also good sources of candidates. You can be sure that the latter have patience and good communication skills.

WHAT TO LOOK FOR IN CLERKS FOR THIS DEPARTMENT

Just as the manager of the customer service department should have certain traits and skills, those who work under him or her should also exhibit characteristics that result in most efficient performance.

In larger companies there are two categories of workers in a customer service department, but desired skills for both groups overlap. They are the adjustment group and the support group; their functions are detailed in Chapter 8.

Staffing the adjustment group

Adjustment personnel must make the actual decision on how a specific communication is handled. These are the traits and skills required for the job:

Good vision and physical dexterity.

Good handwriting and a command of simple written English.

Intelligence and a good memory.

Well spoken and courteous, for those chosen to respond to customers by telephone.

Thoroughness and attention to detail.

Team worker—no "loners" need apply.

Good vision. This basic need—adjusted by proper eyeglasses, if necessary—is required to read the sometimes nearly illegible letters from customers. Physical dexterity and clerical aptitude are mandatory to sort, count, write, and file rapidly and accurately the many pieces of paperwork either received or generated in the customer service function.

Good handwriting. The requirement for clear, legible handwriting goes along with my oft-repeated recommendation that as many queries as possible be handled by a short, handwritten note or by a filled-in form. Obviously, such short responses must be written in understandable English, with emphasis on the *simple.* Those who dote on polysyllabic words are not suited to this task.

There is long-established precedent for this approach to responding. In the early years of Sears, Roebuck and Company, the successful firm's many customers were the source of a heavy flow of correspondence, much of it complimentary but of which a good part had nothing to do with business—they wanted advice on family matters, such as what to name a newborn. Richard Sears insisted that *all* communications with customers be handwritten, until the volume grow so large that typewriters were finally permitted. After both Sears and Alvah Roebuck had retired from the company they founded, they invested in and perfected the Woodstock typewriter.

Intelligence. Although various "decision tables" are part of my approach to responding to customers, considerable judgment is still required of workers in this department. No geniuses need apply (because they would soon be bored with the work), but above-average intelligence, a good memory, common sense, and some "quickness" are highly desirable.

There are plenty of high school graduates who meet these requirements. There is no need to hire college graduates for this work. At first, the "overqualified" college grad may perform very well, and will nearly always learn the job quickly. However, in time they are very likely to get bored with the task and its limited opportunities for advancement, and quit.

I am reminded of the plaint of one executive whose superior had favored college graduates as secretaries, especially if they graduated from one of the "Ivy League" women's colleges (this was in the days before most went co-ed). After the third one in less than two years quit out of sheer boredom, he cried out: "Oh Lord, give me a hungry high school grad."

Well spoken. Obviously, employees who receive or respond to telephone calls from customers should possess clear voices and speak in a pleasant manner. They should also exhibit good telephone manners. If these admonitions appear to belabor the obvious, think back to how often you are annoyed by poor diction and disturbed by the bad manners of a person in a company you only contact by phone. (For example, many individuals are especially offended by the answerer who picks up the phone but continues for a few seconds a prior conversation before speaking.)

To make sure that the employees who are chosen to answer the phone continue to demonstrate the desirable traits for

which they were hired, executives responsible for customer
relations should call their own departments, or, better still,
have someone whose voice is not familiar to your people call
and monitor the telephone manners of your own employees.
A full day's training course on cassettes for telephone order
and customer service clerks is available from Universal Training Systems Co., 3201 Old Glenview Road, Wilmette, Illinois
60091, (312) 251–8700.

Thorough. Because responding to customers involves
much detail, all who work in this department obviously should
be comfortable with and not bored by detail work. They must
be thorough workers, not the kind who push aside communications that are difficult to reply to—and never get back to them.
(Later, in Chapter 8, information is provided on how to set
up controls to make sure that no one ever "permanently
pigeonholes" work.)

Team worker. Because a "team" function is so crucial,
it should be obvious that all employees chosen should be team
workers and not loners. Since a form of competition may develop between the different teams, a somewhat competitive
spirit is also desirable. Even if your operation is not large
enough to require more than one team, the competitive spirit
may manifest itself in the goal of beating last week's performance.

Staffing the support group

Requirements for the employees who back up the personnel
who actually make the decisions on adjustments (the support
group) are very similar to those for the adjustment group.

This is especially true since some of the highest paid workers in the department are those who sort mail, and they come out of the adjustment group. However, some employees in the support group must be able to type competently. This skill is easily determined, either by a test one develops oneself, or by giving a test discussed in the next section. The best reservoir of future adjustment personnel is the support group. Hence, this should be kept in mind when selecting typists, file clerks, and other support clericals. The opportunity to advance makes the hiring of qualified people somewhat easier.

Testing the skills of applicants

Clerical skills are desirable in both categories of employees in the department, so does it make sense to test applicants? Actually, by becoming applicants, they have already taken one test—that for handwriting. If you have difficulty reading the application, and also find that the applicant is confused by the simple directions on the employment application form, then there is no need to proceed further. (If there are many details called for on the application, completing it also reveals if the prospect has a good memory—another desirable trait, as previously mentioned.)

However, if the applicant does have good handwriting, can follow an employment application without difficulty, and also interviews well, you should consider giving the applicants clerical aptitude tests. Such tests have been available for decades. Among the two leading suppliers of such tests are Psychological Corporation, 304 East 45th Street, New York, New York 10017; and E. F. Wonderlic & Associates, Inc.,

P.O. Box 7, Northfield, Illinois 60093. The former, which is now part of Harcourt Brace Jovanovich, Inc., was founded in 1921.

Psychological Corporation offers several clerical tests of varying durations. The longest is the General Clerical Test, which is made up of three parts: clerical speed and accuracy (7 minutes), numerical ability (23 minutes), and verbal facility (17 minutes). The three parts have a total test time of 47 minutes. According to the 1975–76 catalog, this test cost $4.90 for a package of 25, including manual and key; however, a specimen test is available for your evaluation for 90 cents. You don't have to give an applicant all three parts of the test. They are broken into two segments, which can be purchased and given separately.

In addition to these longer tests, Short Employment Tests are also available. These, which are a battery of three five-minute tests, cost only $3.60 for a package of 25 of any one battery.

Wonderlic offers the Hay Clerical Aptitude Tests, which are made up of four parts: the One-Minute Warm-Up, which is not scored, the Number Perception Test, the Name Finding Test, and the Number Series Completion, each of which takes 4 minutes for a total of 15. In packages of 25, this battery of tests costs $15. A sample set costs $4.50. In addition, a Test Administration procedure (with cassette tape) is offered for each of the four parts for $12 each.

Both companies also offer tests that measure stenographic and typing skills. Determining the latter is significant for the support group. However, there is no need to test for steno-graphic skills, since there is little dictation involved—much of the wording of typed responses will be taken from standard paragraphs previously prepared.

All of these tests are discussed in more detail in catalogs available from these two companies. Tests in Spanish also are available for companies that deal with the many millions of Americans whose first language is Spanish.

Do-it-yourself tests

Not all executives who use these tests are happy with them. Muriel G. Adamy, manager of consumer affairs, ITT Continental Baking Co., Rye, New York, created her own test after an applicant who passed one of the professionally prepared tests with flying colors was a complete flop as a worker. Mrs. Adamy's test was quite simple: She asked applicants to compose a short letter in response to a typical complaint.

On-the-job training

Since only a comparatively small number of companies had large customer service departments until recently, there is a limited number of potential employees available who are trained for this specialized work. And even if there were, it is not likely that their experience elsewhere would be transferable to your operation, because customer responses are very much tailored to the needs and function of each company.

Good general training material on how to write effective business letters is to be found in the weekly bulletin called *Letter-Perfect,* a service published by Clement, Inc., Concordville, Pennsylvania 19331. The basic single subscription rate is $2 for each issue. The bulletins cover all aspects of letter writing, from grammar and paragraph structure to how to handle difficult and irritated customers. Another similar service is *Better Letters,* published by The Economics Press, Inc., 12 Daniel Rd., Fairfield, N.J. 07006.

What training comes down to is learning on the job. This should not be too much of a chore if you have chosen alert, intelligent, enthusiastic workers. Training also is very much expedited by the team approach to responding, as detailed in Chapter 8.

chapter 7

Setting policy in customer service

While travelling about the country and working with and visiting dozens of companies each year, I am often struck by a surprising situation. The company either has not set *any* guiding customer service policy, or, if such policy has been set, those employees who must implement it: (*a*) are not aware of rules applying to their jobs, (*b*) are functioning under some superseded rules not in effect for many months or even years, or (*c*) don't know how or where to find out what the applicable policy is.

Now it is not necessary for every employee to memorize a complete book of rules, the way many ship's navigators know the "Rules of the Road," but they should be completely familiar with the few unique rules that pertain to their aspect of the business. And when employees don't know the applicable ground rules, one should not hold them at fault. It's management that is deficient.

If there is any aspect of the business that requires clear, well-implemented policy, it is customer service and communications. Failure to set and implement policy can result in serious losses. This does not mean the merely aggravating delays in answering complaints, although such delays can do much dam-

77

age. It means declines in sales, profits, and hard-won market position!

THE SIX ASPECTS OF POLICY

There are six aspects of the policies that pertain to customer service:

1. Rules that apply directly to the customer, such as "not requiring proof of purchase to adjust items under $25."
2. Standards of performance for the department, such as requiring that all customer communications have a reply initiated "within three working days."
3. Filing standards, that is, deciding what correspondence relating to customers should be retained and for how long. In general, most companies keep too much correspondence too long.
4. Rules on approval. For example, deciding who, by job position, shall approve certain adjustments that exceed the limits set under Rule 1 above.
5. Limitations on changes in procedure—deciding who, by job position, shall approve any changes in procedure; in particular, any changes in form letters sent to customers or consumer advocates.
6. Insuring compliance with any governmental regulations applicable to the company's customer service.

How often should policies be updated?

A policy on review and updating of policy also must be set. Early in the introduction of a new or rehabilitated customer service department, I believe that quarterly policy reviews are called for. However, once the department is established and running smoothly, semiannual or annual reviews are sufficient. There is also the question of the extent to which certain aspects of policy should be publicized. The fact that the company does not require proof of purchase for reshipment of "undelivered" items costing less than, say, $25 need not be revealed either to customers or to staff members, other than those who approve credits or refunds. Otherwise, there is a good chance that the comparatively small number of "ripoff experts" will prey on your company.[1]

Who should participate in policy making and review?

Reviewing policy means that some executives are assigned to the policy committee. An obvious choice is the executive responsible for customer service and, if the company has an ombudsman and he or she is not the customer service manager, this person should also be a member. A representative of the marketing department must participate; perhaps the top marketing executive. Since customer service is involved with return of merchandise, which hopefully can be returned to stock (some of it can't, even if still seasonal), a representative of the distribution function should be assigned to enable the committee to assess the economics of handling returns, exchanges,

[1] In his *Steal This Book,* Abbie Hoffman, the well-known Yippie leader, outlines procedures on page 84 for "ripping off" mail-order book and record clubs and merchants. Preventing the unscrupulous from ever taking advantage of customer-oriented policies is impossible (and very costly in implementation), but it is possible to hold losses from deliberate fraud to a tolerable minimum. *Steal This Book,* 318 pages, was published in 1971 by Pirate Editions, Inc., New York, and sells for $1.95.

and replacements. At the least, the committee should consult with the controller's function on the impact of its policies on the company's overall expenses and profits.

If the review committee is thought of as a sort of "board of directors" for the customer service department, then it might be constituted, as is common with many such boards for corporations, with an *outside* director. This expert could be the head of customer service for some local company, the company's legal counsel, or even the company's consultant on customer service. Just like outside corporate directors, the outside members should be paid an honorarium for participating.

Because a customer service function can have a substantial impact on a company's performance, positive or *negative,* some participation or review by top management makes sense. In smaller operations, the president of the company might well assign himself to this committee, although he should not function as its chairman.

External and internal influences on policy making

There are three major influences in setting customer service policy:

1. The practices in your industry or locality. These comprise an external influence.

2. Another external influence is government—at the municipal, county, state, or federal level, or by the U.S. Postal Service.

3. Internal influences, such as the sales department's obvious desire to maximize sales, the financial executive's proper thrust towards lower overhead costs, and the distribution function's need to hold down inventory. In addition, changes in policy

could result from feedback from the customer service department itself, indicating that existing policy is too rigid or demanding, thus adding unnecessarily to the burden of the department.

Examples of customer service policy

To help the individuals or the committee responsible for setting customer service policy, the following examples illustrate current policy in successful operations dealing with the consumer. (A typical set of customer service policies is shown in Figure 9.)

Taking the customer's word. Obviously, policy must be set for accepting the customer's word that a desired action should be taken. To hold down much back-and-forth correspondence, I always urge clients to set a maximum amount below which *no proof of payment is required* to complete action.

Here are examples of such amounts: $20, $25! If these amounts appear high to you, consider how much it costs you to verify a purchase, or to request that the customer submit proof of purchase, and the high percentage of subsequent replies that offer proper proof of purchase. And don't forget that you are also putting your valued customer to the trouble and expense of obtaining photocopies of the relevant documents. Some companies feel obligated to repay even this expense.

Cash or credit? In implementing the money-back guarantee, companies must decide whether to refund in cash or provide a credit against future purchases. Again, the more liberal policy of implementing the guarantee in cash should be fol-

82

FIGURE 9

An example of codified customer service policies

1. We will *cheerfully* and promptly replace or refund the full purchase price in accordance with the terms of our guarantee: "Our products are guaranteed to be 100 percent satisfactory. Return anything purchased from us that proves otherwise. We will replace it or refund your money, as you wish." Our responsibility is clear—the customer must be *completely satisfied.*

2. We will answer customer correspondence with sufficient speed to insure that our reply is received in the calendar week following the week of customer inquiry. All telephone calls will be returned within two days even if the requested information is not available.

3. We will use the telephone instead of written communications for:
   a. Aggravated complaints.
   b. Mail unanswered for a prolonged period.
   c. In reply to telephone complaints.
   d. To eliminate complicated letters.

4. We will acknowledge all customer communications including:
   a. Cancellations.
   b. Cross in the mail correspondence.
   c. Complimentary letters.

5. We will take customer's word and will reship merchandise if the customer indicates nondelivery two weeks or more after the order should have been shipped, if the customer lives east of the Mississippi; three weeks if the customer lives west of the Mississippi.

6. We will refund returned shipment postage when requested, or when adjusting a serious complaint.

7. We will refund to the penny all amounts due the customer as a result of an overpayment or an adjustment.

8. We will maintain a record of all policy adjustments.

9. We will take the customer's word for all returns and payments involving less than $25.
   a. For payments in excess of $25 we will request a copy of the customer's cancelled check.
   b. For returns in excess of $25 we will request proof of shipment in the form of an insurance receipt.
   c. If an insurance receipt is not available, the case will be reviewed on its merits.

lowed, although the customer can be given the choice of cash or credit.

What should be the proof of purchase when a refund exceeds the minimum? If the refund requested or the complaint of failure to deliver exceeds the stipulated minimum, what proof of purchase should be requested? A copy of the customer's cancelled check or money order receipt is suitable proof. But stress in all forms and correspondence that only a copy is needed. You don't want the responsibility of custody of the customer's actual cancelled check (but some will forward them in spite of urgings to the contrary).

Nondelivery. Both failure to deliver and partial delivery (items missing from a "set") are the most common complaints from customers. What policy should be set for such failures that irk so many customers? Again, the proof-of-purchase test should be applied to nondelivery. If the customer insists that the company did not deliver a $25 pair of shoes, and the company's policy is not to require proof of purchase for items below $30, then you should set a policy that calls for automatic reshipment in response to such requests.

This type of adjustment, where no merchandise is received from the customer, is called a *policy adjustment.* Efficient customer service operations maintain records by customer, either manually or on the computer, for all such adjustments. These records are consulted before a policy adjustment is made to be sure that the customer is not taking unfair advantage.

Some mail-order houses also question claims of "nondelivery" from certain categories of customers who have historically been the source of a suspiciously high number of such claims. Included are: students and others associated with the academic community, persons whose only address is a post office box number, people living overseas, and convicts (who have no other means but mail order for shopping and gift giving). One way to cut down sharply on such claims is to ship to these categories via United Parcel Service, which requires a signature on all deliveries, or to insure items sent parcel post. To also hold down on problems with "difficult" categories, some mail-order firms require payment *prior* to shipment.

Damaged goods. In most instances, the customers will send back the damaged goods. Usually, they will pay the cost of shipment. However, if they return the goods by a means that requires the company to pay the cost of return, or they demand that the company reimburse them for returning the goods, the company should comply with the customers' demands. (This assumes, of course, that the item is of rather compact size and not too heavy. For extremely bulky goods, the company should set up a procedure for inspection at the customer's premises prior to reshipment.) If the reported damage has "destroyed the value of the product," as would be the case with glassware, it is not sensible economically or in terms of good customer relations to have the recipient return items of little value.

Expiration of money-back guarantee or warranty. A common problem is the customer demanding his money back after the expiration of the money-back guarantee or the warranty period. In general, companies should not apply the expiration date too rigidly, especially since many customers actually may not begin using the product on the date of sale, but some time later, such as date of delivery. For instance, one manufacturer of home heating systems replaces its warranted heat exchanger as much as six months after the termination of its ten-year guarantee on this key part.

Where guarantees are involved, sometimes adjustment personnel tend to be too protective of the company. This frequently creates bad relations with customers who take their trade elsewhere.

Some years ago, the president of a mail-order nursery business was confronted with these facts: one of his featured items was a "fruit cocktail tree" that, by means of grafting, grew five separate fruits. He was told that customers were complaining, under the terms of the company's guarantee, that the tree was growing only three or four of the five fruits.

The adjustment clerks were responding that the tree would have to be returned before a new tree could be sent. As a result, the customers were pulling the tree from the ground, packing it, and shipping it to the company's warehouse, where it was carted to the dump—an unnecessary, annoying, and expensive task for everyone! The president stalked out of his office and changed that policy immediately. As in this case, are your customer service people too shortsighted?

Bouquets and brickbats. One category of letter should always be acknowledged: complimentary ones. If someone takes the trouble to sit down and write a compliment, it should definitely be replied to in a formal manner by an executive— or in the name of an executive—of the company. Especially since such laudatory letters will be few and far between.

How to handle another category of complimentary reply: the gift to an employee from an especially pleased customer? Anyone who has taken the trouble to send a gift would be insulted if it were returned. But the recipient of the gift should get assistance in preparing and typing a formal reply, no matter how low in rank the employee.

Companies dealing with consumers should also expect the opposite of compliments—brickbats. As long as the denunciations are in writing, the damage is hard to assess. However, some irate customers have been known to enclose dead insects with their denunciations. (See page 11 for additional examples of extreme reactions.)

Replying to communications by phone. Companies should use the telephone to reply to the following communications:

For aggravated complaints.

To eliminate complicated letters.

In reply to phoned complaints.

For important responses to nearby customers. (Many companies report that it's less costly to use the outwards-WATS service than to compose, type, and mail a letter).

As indicated in Chapter 10, it does not make sense to encourage customers to telephone their complaints, although some companies, as detailed, have gone out of their way to accept phoned-in complaints—because it helped them to find out quickly why they were losing sales or potential customers. Encouraging customers to call on a toll-free "800" inward-WATS number can greatly increase the cost of customer communications; however, it is generally recommended that collect calls be accepted. The volume of such calls is rarely very great. And usually the customer who makes a collect call is pretty mad and takes this step because the company has failed to respond quickly or at all by mail.

Since many telephone calls cannot be handled right away, it's important that all essential information be obtained while the customer is on the line. Use of the Telephone Inquiry Form (shown in Figure 10) has eliminated annoying callbacks to the customer for missing information.

FIGURE 10

Telephone Inquiry

Ms.
Mr.
Mrs. _____   Date _____
Miss.
Street _____   Phone _____

City _____ State _____ Zip _____   Best time _____
                                                          to call

☐ ORDER NOT RECEIVED ☐ BACK ORDER NOT RECEIVED	☐ PAYMENT	☐ REFUND/CREDIT ☐ EXCHANGE
Was order to this address? _____ (If no, write address on back of sheet.)	Amount _____	Return sent _____
	Date mailed _____	Shipped via _____
Date order mailed _____	Pay by check? _____	Insured? _____ Instructions in the box? _____
Pay by check? _____	Check cleared? _____	Return acknowledged? _____
Check cleared? _____		List returned and replacement items below.
Customer wants:		
Items ordered _____	☐ BILLING	☐ MISSING/INCORRECT ITEM
To cancel _____	Describe on back of sheet.	List items below.
A substitute _____		

Have you contacted us before about this? _____ When? _____

Comments _____
_____
_____

Could you give me the order number from the packing list/invoice/acknowledgement? _____

RETURNED/INCORRECT/CANCEL ITEMS			ORDER/REPLACEMENT/MISSING/BACK ORDER ITEMS		
Item No.	Qty.	Description	Item No.	Qty.	Description

Customer was told _____
☐ No further response is necessary.   ☐ Must respond to customer.

Action taken _____ Adjuster _____ Date _____

A detailed telephone inquiry form guides clerks to ask all pertinent questions.

FILING STANDARDS

"File as little as possible" is the best advice. Many companies purchase literally scores of files to store correspondence with customers going back years. But rarely, if ever, is this information referred to again. In one instance, after a company followed the recommendation not to store all this dead information, it didn't have to buy another filing cabinet in the entire business for years because so many were emptied. It also made good use of the valuable floor space devoted to those ranks of file cabinets.

If the company doesn't file customer correspondence, who should? "The customer," is the answer. Return all but routine correspondence to the customer. Unless he's writing from an office, he rarely has kept a copy and will appreciate his original letter to compare the company response. Then, in the rare instance that a dispute arises (less likely when a company institutes a liberal "take-word" policy), ask the customer to forward copies of relevant documents.

This means imposing a cost for copying. Most people seem to have a photocopier available to them—one of the reasons why photocopier suppliers gross so much. If necessary, *reimburse* the customer for making the photocopies. It's much, much cheaper than filing yourself. However, files of original letters and responses to all VIPs (see Chapter 4) should be maintained.

In all my years working in customer service, I find that the elimination of correspondence files is one of—if not the most —difficult customer service policy for management to implement. The clinching point is made when management learns how some concerns (such as the mail-order giants and the book and record clubs) receive upwards of 25,000 letters a week yet maintain only a single file cabinet for VIP correspondence.

RULES ON APPROVAL OF ADJUSTMENTS

Once a maximum figure has been set for taking the customer's word on an adjustment or a request for credit, in my experience the volume of customer contacts will fall off by from 25 percent to 30 percent. How to resolve the remaining fractions? The largest part of the adjustments that exceed the above maximum will fall into a range of dollar amounts about double that of the maximum. Thus, if the "take-word" maximum is $25, most of the remaining adjustments will be from $25 to $75. Resolving adjustments in this range could be left to the discretion of departmental assistants, even of team leaders (see page 105).

Now we are left with a very small number of adjustments involving larger sums. These should be brought to the attention of the head of the department for quick resolution.

LIMITATIONS ON CHANGES IN PROCEDURE

Once policy has been set on a given matter, it should not be changed except at the direction of a responsible executive or by the customer service policy committee. Yet there have been situations in which a low-ranking executive or a clerk may take a shortcut that in effect abrogates policy. The clerk may have made the change in the mistaken belief that he or she is

90

raising efficiency, or to save their own effort. Either way, unilateral action is not to be tolerated.

When a clerk or executive exceeds their authority and makes an unwarranted change in procedure or policy, the reason why the change is unacceptable must be explained to the guilty party. No need to discharge them; they may be well-motivated employees who simply did not realize they were stepping outside their true role.

Limitations on changes in procedure also apply to forms. Again, there are instances in which employees without a true understanding of the importance of all elements in a form letter or postcard have made unwarranted changes, usually at a time when the department ran out of an old form. In general, when stocks of a form long in use are approaching depletion, and new forms must be printed, the head of the department should study the form for possible improvements or updating. However, he or she should be the only person with the authority to make such changes. (See Figure 21.)

COMPLIANCE WITH
GOVERNMENTAL REGULATIONS

The powerful intrusion of government at all levels into relations between businesses and their customers requires careful monitoring of new regulations by the head of the customer service department. When new regulations require changes in procedure in customer communications, they should be made promptly, and only at the direction of the head of the department with the approval of the policy committee and the company's legal counsel, where appropriate.

STANDARDS OF PERFORMANCE

Setting standards of performance for the customer service function is important for two reasons. First, these standards should insure that all queries get a prompt response, thus pleasing the customer. Second, the standards should increase the efficiency of the department, thus holding down on overhead.

Here are some of the standards:

1. All work shall be handled in order of receipt.
2. All correspondence shall be replied to within three working days unless information is not available.
3. Phone queries not resolved by the person who answers the call shall be responded to by phone within 24 hours, unless the call is received the afternoon of the last work day of that week, when the response shall be made by the end of the first work day of the following week.

"Continuity" in customer relations

One other aspect of customer relations that should be discussed as a matter of policy. Many companies with a heavy volume of customer communications assign fictional names to individual correspondents (or to the department head) to maintain continuity to outsiders over the years, and to make it easy for the customer to remember a name to contact. Frequently only a first initial is used, such as E. Brown, in order to eliminate any problem, if a man or woman answers the telephone. This policy makes sense in many situations, although it does represent a minor and quite harmless deception. And use of such a fictional name speeds responses to customers because whenever a letter or phone call is received addressed to that name, everyone understands the nature of the query and it is routed directly to the customer service department.

chapter 8

Structuring a group to handle written or phone communications from customers

The handling of consumer complaints should be swift, personalized, courteous, and as effectively managed as any other function of prime importance to the company, including increased personnel training in the handling of consumer communications, complaint follow-up, and appropriate involvement by senior management.[1]

Everyone exposed to customer contacts should heartily endorse this recommendation made by a group of businessmen, who include the chief executive officers of some of the largest corporations in America. To follow up on it is, in effect, the purpose of this book. Nowhere is the efficiency with which a company handles customer communications more likely to be

---

[1] Recommendation 1 from *Complaints and Remedies*, the report of the Sub-Council on Complaints and Remedies of the National Business Council for Consumer Affairs, October 1972.

affected than in the way it *structures* the department directly concerned.

THE THREE Rs

Customer service functions revolve around three basics, which I call the three Rs: *reading, researching,* and *responding.* Each of these elements is interdependent upon the other, and each must be performed with *precision* and in accordance with *established routines.* If you are able to accomplish this, you will achieve:

Fast turnaround on your customers' inquiries.

Meaningful and accurate responses.

Low operating costs.

In assisting dozens of companies to organize and systematize their customer service departments, I have developed a number of basic *operating* philosophies and techniques that have been proven and tested in both large and small installations. Although these have been designed primarily for the consumer complaints and inquiries resulting from merchandise and publication sales, manufacturers who transact business with dealers and distributors will find them of value, also.

Superior service to the maximum number

To obtain the highest efficiency, I always recommend that companies stress *superior* service to the *maximum number* of people. This does not mean that some fraction of customers is neglected, or that their complaints are set aside or never answered, but that by disposing of as many *simple* communications just about immediately, and in an informal manner, the department will find that it can handle the more serious and more complicated complaints expeditiously as well.

GETTING ORGANIZED TO READ THE MAIL

Whether you receive ten or 10,000 customer contacts a day (and the large catalog houses, book and record clubs, credit card firms, and public utilities receive that latter volume), you must be *structured* to handle them, whether they are letters, phone calls, or returned packages. Here are recommendations on getting organized to read the mail and handle the calls.

1. Centralization of all those responding to customer communications.
2. Dating and control of all incoming mail, and noting and dating of incoming phone conversations as well. Special controls for VIP mail.
3. Assignment of the most experienced and highly paid employees to the sorting of mail.
4. Organization by team and work specialization.
5. Weekly reporting of departmental production and status.
6. Installation of efficient work stations and equipment.

Centralization means efficiency

Some experts believe that customer response can be decentralized to some extent. This is not sound, especially where smaller operations are involved. Even in the case of giant corporations, there is no basic need for branch or regional response operations. Of course, retailers must provide some customer service function at each retail facility of substantial size.

But this is the only exception that makes any sense. With nationwide mail and phone service, and the feasibility of direct contact to the company's computer from any location, there is no reason why all responses to customer complaints and communications can't be handled from one location. However, it is not essential for a very large company to house its customer response group in the same building, or even in the same city, as company headquarters. Floor space is very costly, usually, in corporate headquarters buildings. Air-conditioned, neat, clean, modern, or at least very well-kept, quarters are quite satisfactory.

Consideration of suburban and retired workers. Since there may be a need to draw on temporary help to cope with seasonal peaks (as suggested in Chapter 6), a suburban location may be preferable on this count alone. The suburbs are well populated with housewives seeking a bit of extra income, or who welcome a chance to get out of their homes during the hours when their children are in school. Many of these women have held responsible jobs prior to childbearing and are quickly trained in the department's work.

In addition to local housewives, another good source of temporary workers that every cost-conscious company should consider is retirees. As long as the extra income gained does not exceed a certain limit—approximately $2,520 per year—these willing and experienced retired workers do not suffer any dimunition in their social security payments. And beyond the age of 72, there is no loss of benefits no matter how much regular income a retiree takes in. Some retirees may even be willing to suffer some dimunition in benefits prior to reaching age 72 simply to keep busy or to maintain their income in the face of continued inflation.

Suburban location simplifies overtime hours. There is another reason why a suburban location is desirable. It's the time of a heavy load of communications, when employees may be asked to stay a few hours late to get out the bulk of responses that do not fall into that "complex" category requiring additional research. In general, it is less burdensome to stay an hour or two late in the suburbs than in some central city location, where public transportation drops off sharply in frequency after rush hours and the element of danger to a person increases.

Customers will have no trouble finding the address and phone number of the response group if the company follows the now standard and intelligent practice of prominently listing this information in catalogs, on order forms, and on packing slips.

The rare communication that is addressed directly to the president of the company can be routed quickly enough to the response group for timely action, and within the week-after rule.

Dating of all mail by colored tags

All letters and phone communications should be dated, either by hand or electric stamping. Experience has shown that the customer expects to receive a reply in the calendar week following the one in which he or she wrote to a company. They are not likely to remember the exact day on which they wrote (unless they kept a carbon of a typed communication, a growing practice among sophisticated consumers). However, they do remember the week.

To stay within the week-after time limit, only a few days

FIGURE 11

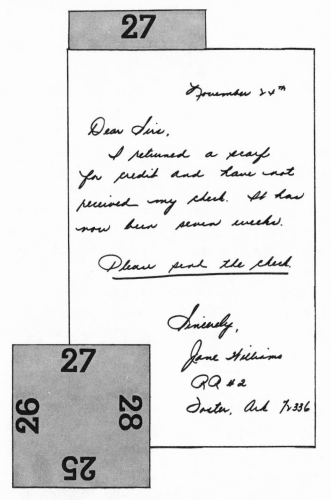

Color-coded date tag and illustration of correspondence, with a tag attached.

are left for processing if return time is counted. Fortunately, the Postal Service is now routing all first class mail by air when it has to travel any great distance.

The most effective way to date incoming communications is to staple a color-coded date tag at the top. These tags (samples of which are illustrated in Figure 11) are three inches square. One side of the square sticks up, and this side shows the current date of the month. A different color is assigned to each span of four days. By this means, a clerk can quickly segregate a stack of mail into sequence by date, either for processing or counting. And the color coding makes it very easy for a supervisor to spot "stale" mail in passing, without having to riffle through a pile of letters. These tags can be ordered from any letter shop or be prepared in your company's own print shop.

The secret is in the "sort"

If there is any one aspect of structuring a response group that has to be emphasized, it is the importance of the "sort." Because most companies assign their youngest, most-recently hired and lowest-paid employees to the mailroom, it is sometimes difficult to get across the notion that for maximum efficiency the employees assigned to the sorting of mail in the customer service department should be among the most experienced and best-paid workers in the group. Any executive experienced in handling customer communications will confirm this strong recommendation.

Using a multiple-position sorting rack (similar to the one illustrated in Figure 12) the sorters should segregate mail, based on their complete familiarity with it, into three major categories: *simple, medium,* and *complex,* including complaints

FIGURE 12

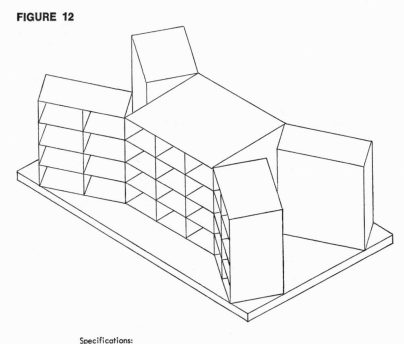

Specifications:

1. Compartments 9½" wide X 5½" high X 12" deep.
2. Top, bottom, sides and vertical separators - ½" plywood.
3. Shelves - ¼" Masonite.
4. Table size 66" X 48".

Two sorters can work simultaneously at this sorting rack.

from VIPs. This can be accomplished easily by a quick *scanning* of the letter. There is no need to take the time to *read* the letters.

Most communications fall into the simple category—between 55 and 65 percent. Since the majority of communications in the simple category require little if any researching, and usually can be answered by form letter, or informally in one or two sentences, it should be obvious why sorting is so crucial to the concept of providing superior service to the maximum number of people.

Beyond the breakdown into the three major categories, each one is further segregated into subcategories. (A typical listing of such sort categories is shown in Figure 13.) Who takes the sorted mail from the sorting rack to the work tables? The supervisor could do this in a small operation, since he or she should be moving about the operation in the normal course of the work day. In larger operations, the team leader could pick up work in batches as his or her fellow team members finish processing prior batches.

One other point should be emphasized about sorting: start early. If your response group is indeed as efficient as many others have become, then the greatest part of the incoming mail will be answered within the day—and most of the employees in the adjustment group will finish with *clean desks* at the end of their working day. To maintain efficiency and productivity, fresh batches of communications should be presented to them or placed in their "in" baskets *before* they arrive at work each day.

Obviously, the sorters have to start before the adjusters. In the most efficient operations this means that the sorters report to work before the commencement of normal working hours. For example, at Doubleday's big book fulfillment operation in Garden City, N.Y., the sorters start work at 7 A.M., 75 minutes before the adjusters. Doubleday has a very heavy volume of incoming mail because it operates so many book clubs. Your operation may not require a 75-minute head start for sorters; an hour or 45 minutes may be sufficient.

However, there may be some obstacle that prevents your opening the office from 45 to 90 minutes early for the sorters to begin work. Or you may be unable to recruit enough sorters to work early (this is unlikely); if such is the case, then the work load should be so arranged that some adjusting work is

102

FIGURE 13

Sample "sort" categories

Simple

1. Product Information
   Is size/color/style
      available?
   Do you carry
      the item?

2. Order Information
   How do I order?
   What are the credit
      options?
   How do I
      exchange?

3. Fulfillment Problems
   Item omitted
   Received in error
   Wrong quantity
   Damaged merchandise

4. Customer List
   Change address
   Put on mailing list
   Take off mailing list

5. Order/Back Order Problems
   Order not received
   Where is back order?
   Cancel back order

Medium

6. Order Processing Problems
   Billed twice
   Not given sale price
   Billed recipient of gift

7. Payment Problems
   Claims paid
   Account credited for wrong
      amount

8. Returns and Exchange Problems
   Replacement not received
   Refund not received
   Wrong replacement
   Wrong amount of refund

Complex

9. Second Complaints
   Received no answer
   Misinterpreted my letter

10. Multiple Problems
   Order sent to wrong customer
   Long, involved letters

11. VIP
   Attorneys, BBB, DMMA, and
      similar agencies
   Postal Service and governmental agencies
   Consumer advocates and
      the media

left over for the following day, until the sorters have generated a few batches for the adjusters. There is nothing sacred in the concept of the clean desk, except on the last work day of the week!

In a very small operation, or when you are launching a response group, the working supervisor is usually assigned the job of sorting—until this chore becomes so demanding that the supervisor can't supervise properly.

What is the range of production for sorters? Trained sorters can sort about 100 to 200 letters per hour.

The "team" concept

The next most significant recommendation, after the experienced sorters, is to group employees of the adjustment category into teams. The teams could vary in size from two or three up to six or seven, but generally the three-person team is most efficient. (A typical organization plan is shown in Figure 14.) These are the advantages of the team approach:

1. Team members can be assigned work on the basis of complexity, and thereby become *specialists* in certain categories of problems.

2. Because the lead member of the team is also the supervisor of the group, close supervision is attained, especially since all members of the team sit side by side at the same worktable. The team leader is available to answer questions and to review finished work from time to time, thus assuring responses of high quality and conformance to established policies.

3. It is easy to provide on-the-job training by means of the team approach and the close physical proximity of its mem-

FIGURE 14

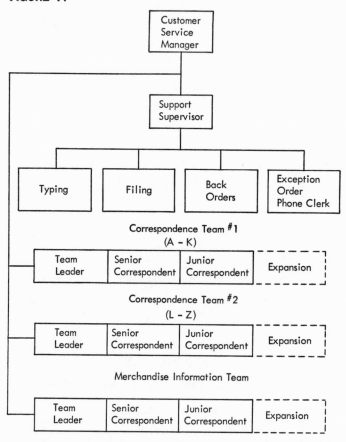

Organization of the customer service department of a medium-to-large company.

bers. New and inexperienced employees should be assigned only simple categories.

4. Where the operation deals with a volume of communications heavy enough to justify setting up more than one team, a team spirit can be developed, with competition between teams that results in even higher productivity.

5. Work measurement is simplified—productivity is reported by team.

6. If there are seasonal peaks in the volume of incoming communications, which is often the case, the team can function as a cadre and be expanded by temporary workers to cope with such peaks. Thus, a two- or three-person team can be expanded in the peak season to include one or two temporary workers, with little decline in efficiency per worker because of the close supervision inherent in the concept.

7. Finally, and significantly, it provides an evident path for promotion.

Functions of the members of the team

How should the work be divided among the members of the team? If the team is made up of the optimum number, three, here is a suggested breakdown of function:

The *team leader* is responsible for:

1. Maintaining work flow and work quality.
2. Keeping team records.
3. Training new personnel and answering questions.
4. Handling complex complaints and those from VIPs.
5. Dictating complex letters.
6. Calling customers on complex problems.

The *senior correspondent* specializes in:

1. Performing research on "medium category" problems and responding with form letters and form responses.
2. Answering the telephone and recording the customer's inquiry if it cannot be immediately answered.
3. Assisting the team leader with complex problems.

The *junior correspondent* is charged with the following:

1. Handling simple problems using decision tables, and filling in the form letters and cards.
2. Creating "internal action" documents to correct records when this is required.
3. Maintaining the form supplies, the form notebook, and any required files.

How to divide the work. A single team should be able to handle all the communications received by a smaller organization from its customers. However, larger companies with a heavy volume of mail have to devise some rational and equitable basis for dividing the work among teams when more than one team is needed. In the past, bases for division have included:

By state or region, such as East, Midwest, and West.

By account number, which is a very simple way to divide.

By the alphabet, using the last name, another simple approach.

An alternative to the team. Although a strong believer in the team approach, I am aware of some highly efficient response operations that are not organized into teams. These operations assign to clerks work that is based on the nature of the problem. For example, one major magazine publisher has identified no less than 48 different problem areas in subscriber communications, and it segregates incoming mail on this basis. Clerks working individually can become experts on a specific problem. Thus, there is only a need to train each adjustment clerk in a specific problem, and there is no need for extensive training in all the problems encountered.

Each organization has to decide for itself, based on the volume and complexity of incoming communications, which approach is superior. However, if you find that the approach taken, either team or individual, is not working well, don't hesitate to switch to the other. It will not entail any great investment in equipment or retraining.

Informal and formal methods of reporting production

For proper functioning, and to maintain productivity, the output of the department must be measured and recorded. There are two approaches for measuring and recording: informal and formal.

Informal. When this approach is taken, the individual employee maintains his or her own production records and reports output on a daily basis to the team leader.

This approach is preferable in a customer service operation because it generates a higher level of employee responsibility and makes the employee feel more important and trusted. Obviously, it also calls for less supervisory effort. The informal method is particularly well suited to the smaller operation.

Formal. In very large operations (some response groups total over 100 employees), where there is high employee turnover (perhaps because many temporaries are brought in to meet seasonal peaks), or where other reasons invalidate the informal reporting method, obviously the formal approach must be taken.

Under this approach, standards of productivity are determined for each category of work, and work is assigned to clerks and recorded by a sign-out clerk, who maintains the records of output. In operations where formal work measurement systems have been installed, labor costs have dropped as much as one-third, in comparison with the prior no-measurement approach.

No matter which approach you take—and this should be determined by experience, and by observing response groups similar in size and function to yours—weekly production records should be maintained for each employee in the department. The mere maintenance of such records tends to improve productivity and, of course, they are of inestimable value at the time of salary reviews.

Weekly operations control report

The color-coded date tags and a weekly operations control report are the key control elements to provide fast turnaround service. (A typical customer service operating control report is shown in Figure 15.) The report provides four important types of information:

1. The amount of correspondence and telephone calls received and handled during the week.

2. An aged physical inventory of the letters/telephone inquiries on hand and unanswered at the close of business on Friday. This can be done, utilizing the color-coded date tags previously discussed. (Some large and well-run customer service functions take a physical inventory of incompleted work at the end of every day.)

3. Processing-time data, which tells the average number of days it has taken to handle a typical letter during the week.

4. The productivity of the department, in comparison with budget.

FIGURE 15

CUSTOMER SERVICE OPERATING CONTROL REPORT

Week ending _____

WORKLOAD SUMMARY					
Day	Starting carryover	Correspondence—Recorded phone calls			Phone calls completely handled
		Received	Processed	Carryover	
Monday					
Tuesday					
Wednesday					
Thursday					
Friday					
Saturday					
Total					

SERVICE CONTROL				
Actual aged carryover		Processing time		
Day received	Quantity		Total pieces sampled	Average days
Previous—Over 5 days				
Monday		Correspondence _____		
Tuesday				
Wednesday		Oldest 5 percent of		
Thursday		above sample _____		
Friday		Recorded telephone _____		
Total on hand		calls		

PRODUCTIVITY CONTROL					
Units processed per worker-hour					
This week		Year to date		Previous year	
Budget	Actual	Budget	Actual	Budget	Actual

Control report for a customer service department.

In some companies the weekly report also includes a tabulation of the mail and phone communications by problem. Such records are not required on a continual basis. Since the pattern of problems changes gradually, a sample tabulation should be made about once a month for the various types of problems. This has proven to be adequate, and it eliminates the need for comprehensive recording and summarizing by problem for regular weekly reporting.

Work stations promote efficiency

Properly designed work arrangements for customer service personnel provide these advantages:

Increased worker efficiency.

Better work control.

Easier training.

Reduced equipment needs, such as for computer terminals and microfiche viewers.

Worktables *without drawers* are best for customer service. Tables, of course, are less expensive than desks and the lack of drawers prevents work from being mislaid or hidden.[1] Hooks can be installed under the worktable to hold pocketbooks, and the increased leg room saves many a pair of hose.

Team arrangements can vary with the number of members and the equipment required. (The illustrations in Figure 16

---

[1] This is not unusual, as proven by an incident at a prominent magazine publisher. After an assistant in the subscription department was discharged for cause, inspection of her desk revealed a hoard of unanswered correspondence from subscribers dating back more than six months.

FIGURE 16

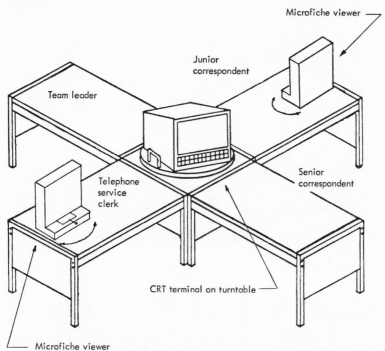

Work station with a CRT (cathode-ray tube) terminal mounted on a Lazy Susan to make it easily available to each member of the four-person team.

and 17 show possible layouts for three- and four-person teams. In both examples, equipment such as viewers and cathode-ray tube (CRT) units not being used continually are shared by two or more of the team members.)

Neatness is a key to efficiency. Hence, work stations should have the proverbial "place for everything . . . and everything should be in place," including storage arrangements for work in process, response forms, and research tools.

FIGURE 17

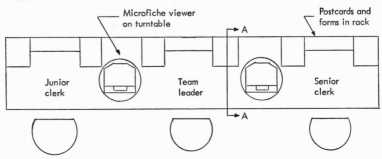

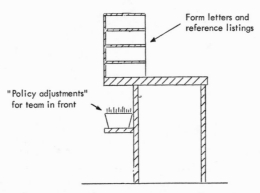

Section A – A

Three-person work station with cross-sectional view showing location of the research files that are referred to frequently.

THE SECOND R—RESEARCHING

If reading, specifically scan-reading, and sorting the incoming mail is performed by an experienced worker, the mail will be broken down into meaningful sort categories. Except for a number of simple categories, the next task is to *research* the information needed to reply to the customer. The correspondent

responsible for making decisions must have these basic reference tools:

1. Copy of the written basic adjustment policies to be followed.
2. Decision tables comprising sample problems encountered,
   action to be taken, and response to be used. (See Figure
   18.)
3. Notebook with samples of all form letters, postcards, and
   form paragraphs, and examples of how each is to be used.
4. Merchandise information sources that provide data on:
   prices; operation, use, and details of products; inventory
   status; repair service; replacement parts; and names of
   local dealers.
5. Organized files or fast look-up records on the following
   (discussed subsequently in further detail) :

   policy adjustments.

   order and shipping information.

   accounts receivable.

   returned goods.

   important previous correspondence.

File of all "policy" adjustments. There are two good
reasons for maintaining a file—in alphabetical order, of course
—of all adjustments made according to "policy." In other
words, where the customer's word is taken that he or she did
make a purchase and the goods received were incomplete or
damaged, or not at all. First, the customer may raise some question about the adjustment. Second, this is an aspect of your
business that is subject to *customer fraud.* If the same customer
keeps on claiming "no delivery" or "damaged on arrival," it

FIGURE 18

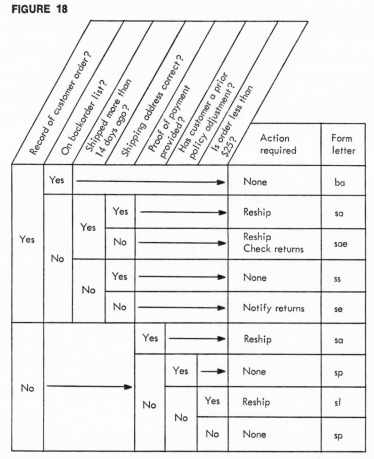

								Action required	Form letter
	Yes						→	None	ba
Yes	No	Yes	Yes				→	Reship	sa
			No				→	Reship Check returns	sae
		No	Yes				→	None	ss
			No				→	Notify returns	se
No				Yes			→	Reship	sa
				No	Yes		→	None	sp
					No	Yes	Reship	sl
						No	None	sp

"Decision table" showing how to research the question, "Where's my order?"

is reasonable to assume that he or she is taking advantage of your customer-oriented policies on adjustment. To detect such larcenous customers, the policy file must be maintained for at least a year.

The file can only be used to detect the unscrupulous customer who uses his own name over and over again to defraud. If he or she uses aliases, or works through others, the file will be of little use in detecting them. Of course, the policy adjustments can also be maintained as a part of the customer's computer record.

Order and shipping information

To perform its work, the adjustment group usually does not need to inspect the actual (original) order, just obtain a confirmation of the fact that the order was indeed received and shipped. How can such confirmations be provided quickly in a reasonably up-to-date form, and preferably, in compact and low-cost form?

If your company is computerized, and this includes data processing by an outside service bureau, you could create a computer output microfilm (COM) index of essential order information. (This is discussed in further detail in Chapter 9.) Another and more economical alternative is to create an alphabetical order index that provides the following basic information on each order:

Name and address of customer.

Order and invoice number.

Date processed.

Dollar value.

Batch number.

The order index frequently provides enough information for the adjustment group to field many queries from customers, particularly the queries pertaining to shipping information. If the query calls for study of the customer's original order or the invoice, the index indicates how to find it quickly, even if a batch filing system is employed.

If you are not computerized, reference frequently must be made to alphabetical customer files containing original orders, invoices, and refunds. These files must be kept current if they are to be of assistance to correspondents in researching customer inquiries.

Accounts receivable file

A common query from customers is, "How much do I owe?" This is one question that often comes in by phone. To resolve this query and others, such as:

"My bill is in error."

"I have been billed twice for an item."

"I have already paid your invoice."

"How did you calculate the handling charges?"

the adjusters must have an accounts receivable file close at hand. Preferably, this should be a computer terminal. If not possible, a current microfilm, a hard-copy computer printout, or an access to the open accounts receivable records would have to be provided.

Returned-goods file

This file should consist of two elements:

1. An alphabetical file of customer letters pertaining to returned goods not yet received.
2. Returned-goods tickets covering merchandise received without instructions. This is a common problem.

Important previous correspondence file

Originals and custom replies to VIP letters, serious complaints (such as those dealing with the safety of products or a large sum of money), and complex problems should be maintained in an alphabetical file. These should be maintained for a year.

RESPONDING—FORMAL AND INFORMAL

A common misconception is that a personalized *typed* letter, even if it is created on a word processing machine, is most respected and appreciated by the customer. The important

FIGURE 19

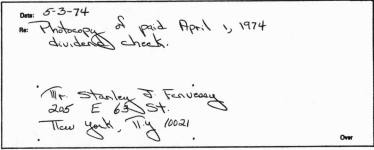

Informality can even be appropriate for simple replies to stockholders, as shown in this example from Ma Bell.

factors are a speedy response and the correct information, not necessarily personally typed. Carefully composed and appropriate form letters—even with handwritten fill-ins—are just as appreciated as personally dictated letters. In fact, such corporate giants as American Telephone & Telegraph employ hand-addressed forms in responding to shareholders (as illustrated in Figure 19). After all, isn't handwriting the ultimate in personalization?

From 75 to 90 percent of all customer inquiries can be answered using preprinted forms adding only addresses and minor fill-ins. Based upon typical clerical production rates, shown below, a form letter can be prepared in: (*a*) less than 10 percent of the time (and at less than 10 percent of the cost) of a dictated and typed personal letter; or (*b*) less than 25 percent of the time of a letter directly typed by the originator.

It is helpful to have at least one form letter or preprinted

FIGURE 20

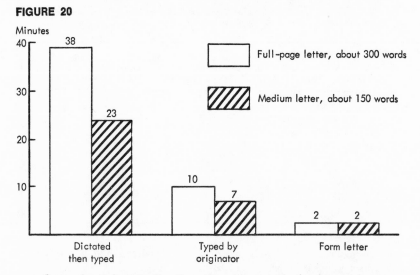

Comparison of production times for various methods of preparing correspondence.

postcard for each major category of problems. A prepared form can be used to answer a number of problems within a category by inserting prepared paragraphs. However, I strongly resist form letters that list many problems in a "laundry list" fashion in which the adjuster checks off the appropriate response. Such a listing tends to scare off customers by showing all the possible pitfalls that could occur in the future if they deal with your company.

Good, clear and easy-to-use form letters just don't happen. They result from a considered analysis of the requirements and a careful development of a total form letter structure. The checklist in Figure 21 should allow you to judge the quality of both your overall program and your individual form letters.

Processing responses

Here are some suggestions to speed up processing and to save time and money:

1. Use printed postcards when a card can handle the problem completely.
2. Use a double or "turnaround" postcard with spaces to fill in and questions to check off. It's effective and economical, if little information is required from the customer.
3. Enclose a return envelope addressed to the customer service clerk when requesting papers or confidential information.
4. Use window envelopes to eliminate the typing of envelopes.
5. Eliminate the use of postcards to acknowledge correspondence. The average customer doesn't appreciate a card

FIGURE 21

Form letter checklist

	Yes	No

Overall program

1. Does each correspondent have a sample form notebook explaining the use and intent of each form? ⎯ ⎯

2. Does each *new* form letter/card follow an approval procedure before it is put into use? ⎯ ⎯

3. Are correspondents trained to discover typed letters that might be replaced with forms? ⎯ ⎯

4. Is there a regular routine for reviewing and re-evaluating *existing* forms? ⎯ ⎯

5. Are systematic controls in effect to insure adequate forms in stock? ⎯ ⎯

6. Is there a meaningful form letter/card numbering system? ⎯ ⎯

Individual forms

1. Is the form businesslike and attractive in appearance? ⎯ ⎯

2. Can the message be understood on the first reading? ⎯ ⎯

3. Is the form letter properly designed for *either* handwritten or typed fill-ins and entry of name, address, and salutation? ⎯ ⎯

4. Is the wording friendly (and sympathetic, if appropriate), yet free of hackneyed cliches? ⎯ ⎯

5. Is the form designed for insertion in a window envelope? ⎯ ⎯

6. Is there space for a personal signature? ⎯ ⎯

7. If the message is brief, is the form a postcard? ⎯ ⎯

8. If a postcard, is the message free of confidential or personal data? ⎯ ⎯

9. Does the form have an identification number? ⎯ ⎯

The questions are worded so that check marks in the *"No"* column indicate the need for corrective action.

telling him that his problem is being worked on—unless, of course, you are temporarily swamped and won't be able to answer for over three weeks.

6. Where the answer is simple, respond in handwriting on the customer's letter. Staple a notation similar to the illustration in Figure 22.

FIGURE 22

INSTANT REPLY

Please excuse our form. We thought you would prefer a speedy reply to a formal letter. Our reply is at the bottom of your letter.

Explanatory form to be stapled to customer letter when it is returned to customer with a handwritten response.

Source: V. W. Eimicke Associates, Inc., Bronxville, N.Y. 10708.

7. Return the customer's letter with your form response. It will be appreciated, and it should help the customer recall his or her problem and, of course, this eliminates filing at your office.

Direct handling

To pursue the philosophy of *superior* service to the maximum number of people, the simple technique that I call "direct handling" must be employed. Only with this approach can responses be answered the same day when received or the next day. Here is what must be done:

1. Fill-in and address in handwriting the form postcard or

letter at the same time that the decision is made. Do not forward the correspondence to another clerk for typing. In fact, the letter should be folded and inserted in the window envelope so as not to require any further handling except delivery to the post office.

FIGURE 23

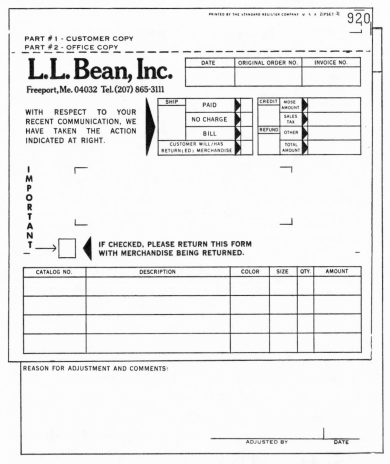

Two-part Service Action form that informs both the customer and the responsible department of the action to be taken.

2. Where internal action, such as adjusting the customer's account, preparing a refund, or reshipping merchandise is called for, complete a Service Action form that, in one writing will both: (a) inform the customer and (b) direct other departments to take the required internal action. (See the example of a two-part Service Action form in Figure 23, used by L. L. Bean, Inc., Freeport, Maine, the nationally famous supplier to outdoorsmen.)

3. If the customer is aggravated, or the complaint complex, use the telephone. The goodwill generated is simply amazing and the company will save money in the long run.

TEST YOURSELF

In the *Guide to Effective Complaint Management,* issued by the President's National Business Council for Consumer Affairs (see Page 2), it is stated that senior management should regularly review samples of actual complaints, and have personal contact with consumers and grievances. Don't let this important image-building function drift without periodic internal review.

Also, a regular and continuing program of testing the customer response department should be undertaken. Wives and husbands or relatives of employees can initiate test orders, or the names of volunteer participants for such a program can be obtained from the Direct Mail/Marketing Association, 6 East 43rd Street, New York, New York 10017.

The results of these two investigations should give you a realistic insight into whether your group is properly structured to handle the written and phone communications from your present and future customers.

RECOMMENDED READING

Consumer Affairs Department: Organization and Functions, by The Conference Board, Inc., 845 Third Avenue, New York, New York 10022, 1973, 114 pages. Available at $17.50 to nonassociate members, and for $3.50 to associate members and those in education.

chapter 9

The role of high technology in improving communications with customers

"Boobtubeitis," that fascination with the TV screen we experienced after World War II, is infecting many parts of business and industry. Now that the cost of computer systems has dropped so rapidly and their capability has expanded commensurately, many organizations are installing TV-like terminals to "talk" to their computers.

When properly specified, a terminal with a cathode-ray tube (CRT) can be a powerful tool for speeding up and expediting data handling operations. However, the availability of such terminals at comparatively low prices—only a few thousand dollars apiece, installed—has resulted in some needless applications of the machines. Managers, who have but rare need for "instant" information, have had CRT terminals installed at their desks. For the rare rush query, they could simply call up some subordinate working at the terminal and request the information over the phone. Obviously, the CRT terminal in such situations adds more to the manager's ego than it adds to company profits.

125

126

Some companies with big computers capable of handling many CRT terminals have had additional banks of these terminals installed for handling communications with customers. In some situations, this helps to justify the original huge investment in the computer.[1]

Companies should not be so carried away by technology that they apply it where it makes but a marginal contribution—or none at all. And all at a very high cost, both in terms of dollars and executive time expended, which often is not calculated into the cost of some technical expansion.

For the purpose of communicating with customers, the *simplest* and *lowest cost* devices and approaches should be applied first. If these simpler concepts fail to achieve the desired speed or effectiveness of response, then, and only then, should more sophisticated technical approaches be considered. First, however, make sure that the organization really requires such a speedy response.

The simplest of approaches are more than adequate. The color-coded date tags (discussed in Chapter 8) are a most powerful tool in expediting responses. Yet, the tags cost only pennies per thousand.

Instead of elaborate word processing systems, ball-point pens at 19 cents apiece in the hands of clerks schooled in good penmanship provide the means of quickly turning out concise responses that are well received by the vast majority of customers.

---

[1] If you are looking for new applications for computers, one of the most productive for high-volume shippers is to obtain permission from the U.S. Postal Service to pay the charges for parcel post on a "computed" basis rather than by use of postage meters. The USPS is prepared to accept figures totaled by the company's computer. The annual fee for participating in this cost-cutting program is $600, and a shipper has to ship at least $200,000 worth of zone-rated parcels via parcel post each year to qualify.

Careful sorting of incoming communications by intelligent, well-trained clerks is the basis of all response systems. No computer yet devised can handle this crucial step in responding. And when decades hence such a computer is developed, you can be sure that it will cost far more than the training of clerks.

Even inward-WATS lines, which are a great advance in telephone communications, are not needed, in my estimation, in a vast majority of cases (see Chapter 10). When a company discontinues its inward-WATS lines for customer complaints, the volume of such communications usually drops by about a third, meaning a big saving in overhead. However, companies should accept collect calls from irate customers. The total cost per month of such calls is small compared to inward-WATS.

Why CRT terminals may not be required

The reason there is only a limited need for CRT terminals is that absolute freshness of data on which decisions must be made in responding to customer communications is not required in most situations. About 80 percent of all customer communications can be fielded with data one to five weeks old. Now there is obviously no need for instant access to a computerized data bank if the relevant data need not be up to the minute. In contrast, CRT terminals are perfectly applied in airline reservation systems where data that is ten seconds old may be out of date, as in the availability of the last unassigned seat on a cross-country flight.

However, if yours is one of the rare companies that decides it needs sophisticated computer terminals to expedite responses to customers (hopefully just those who phone in their complaints), there are ways to make do with fewer terminals.

First, attempt to field the complaint by assigning it to clerks with access to microfiche viewers (discussed in detail later in this chapter). If the data on microfiche are not sufficiently up-to-date, then the call can be transferred to a clerk who has access to the CRT tube (this won't happen very often).

Second, mount the CRT terminal on a Lazy Susan between two, three, or even four clerks working at adjacent desks. Thus, each will have easy access to the fast-response terminal (see Figure 16 in Chapter 8). It is unlikely that the rate of incoming communications needing fast responses would ever require that each clerk be assigned to a separate terminal.

APPLYING WORD PROCESSING
TO CUSTOMER COMMUNICATIONS

Word processing, like the CRT terminal, is very much in vogue these days in the business world. However, it only has limited application when it comes to mass customer communications or to routine responses. Nevertheless, when a company has set up an expensive word processing center, correspondence with the VIPs (as discussed in Chapter 4) could be processed on such machines.

Word processing has been around for many years, ever since the introduction of the automatic typewriter, an example of which is the Auto-Typist. However, the automatic typewriter, which in its earliest form was controlled by holes punched in rolls of paper, like the player piano, is a rather inflexible machine. It can turn out rapidly and cheaply many letters of a promotional nature with the same content. But it cannot handle individually composed letters.

That's where the newer word processors shine. The first modern word processor was introduced by IBM in 1964, based on development work going back at least a dozen years before the introduction of the Magnetic-Tape Selectric Typewriter, the well-known MTST. The MTST was particularly well adapted to the preparation of long documents containing much boiler-plate, those lengthy passages of legal text. Law firms found that the MTST was ideal for long contracts containing many standard legal paragraphs, all "memorized" on the long rolls of magnetic tape that guide the machine in its automatic phase. Since the location of the required paragraphs is known by number, all that it takes to compose a long contract is to indicate which paragraphs are required. Text especially composed for that contract is, of course, typed in the conventional manner. Lawyers remain among the leading users of word processing.

Word processing began with so-called stand-alone machines, the self-contained machines that include the three main elements in word processing: the printing mechanism, the memory, and the control electronics. The prices of these machines keep on dropping. IBM now offers the Memory Typewriter at only $5,400, while Ty-Data, Inc., has introduced the Easy-Writer for attachment to the Selectric typewriter. It costs only $3,995. As newer machines are introduced, older machines become available at attractive used prices. A specialist in used machines is Word Processing Exchange, Inc., 3960 Varsity Drive, Ann Arbor, Michigan 48104. About 1970, more complicated systems began to appear.

Where a very heavy level of correspondence is maintained, it appeared to make sense to "time-share" the memory and control electronics. As a result, such systems as the Accutext made by Comptek, Inc., the Astrocomp from Information Control Systems, Inc., the Computext made by LCS Corporation, and the Wordstream III from Avionic Products Engineering Corporation have been introduced, in which a single larger tape drive, disk, or "diskette" associated control electronics are shared by a number of typing stations.

A further advance is to attach a high-speed printer with a typewriter-like character set to the system for very fast printout of the letters as finally approved. When this is done, the typewriter terminals attached to the system are used just for input and rarely for the automatic typing of the final documents, although they remain capable of that function in case the high-speed printer is out of service or fully occupied.

The most sophisticated of all word processor systems is one in which the company's main central computer is programmed to handle correspondence, with each computer terminal acting as an input and updating device. Only the largest of organizations, such as big insurance carriers, have advanced to this stage. It requires considerable programming skill. An example is the Colonial Penn Insurance Company of Philadelphia.

With the wide availability of computer systems designed especially for smaller companies, it's not surprising to find that programs have been developed that provide word processing on such small systems, even on "intelligent" terminals that work with remote giant computers. For example, a New York-based programming supplier—Base, Inc., of 437 Madison Avenue, New York, N.Y. 10017—is offering a word processing program that runs on the Datapoint 2200, a table-top machine that can operate either as a stand-alone small computer system or as a terminal. The program was originally developed by Ebasco Services, Inc., where it was used to replace MTSTs. Called Cytex-5, the program rents for $100 per month per station. Presumably, word processing programs could be developed for the many small computer systems and terminals now on the market. However, they must have a printer with a typewriter-like character set and not just the matrix printers commonly used with these low-cost systems.

The latest trend in word processing is the introduction of the CRT. These more sophisticated devices cost about twice as much as those based on a standard typewriter. Instead of creating or editing the original document on paper, a page at a time is projected on the TV screen, where it is very easy to correct or modify. The final document is prepared on a printing mechanism without a keyboard, usually one of the new, higher speed "daisy-wheel" printers, which are about twice as fast as the IBM Selectrics that are still used on the vast majority of stand-alone machines. (Actually, a prototype CRT word processor was shown at the 1970 computer show, but the manufacturer of the $25,000 machine soon went out of business. Then after a hiatus of several years, word processors with CRTs reappeared.) Suppliers of machines with CRTs include Linolex Systems, Inc., recently acquired by the 3M Company, and Vydek, Inc. The machines rent for over $400 per month. If you can't directly justify a word processor for correspondence, you should be aware that some models can be so adapted that they also function as Telex terminals.

COMPUTER OUTPUT MICROFILM (COM)

One category of advanced technology does have a place in customer communications. It is computer output microfilm, popularly known by its initials, COM. This is a technique for rapidly creating microfilm or microfiche records from information stored in a computer, without the usual intermediate step of printing on paper for photography.[2] The machines that accomplish this "write" directly on the film that becomes the negative, either by means of streams of electrons or by photographing characters on a CRT. Speed is a result of forming letters at electronic speeds, rather than the mechanical speeds of printers. Since a narrow roll of film can be moved far faster than a wide roll of paper, the process is very fast. The machines, of which there are a half-dozen or so manufacturers, are in the $100,000 range. In addition, subsidiary machines are required to produce copies from the master.

In COM the words "negative" and "positive" copies are somewhat confusing. Actually, the original copy that is made consists of black letters formed on a clear background. The copies made from the original are generally reversed and become white letters on a black background.

Either copy can be used in a viewer. The white letters on a dark background generally are preferred, because there is less glare and a person's eyes usually are more relaxed looking at the darker screen.

The subsidiary machines that are the biggest irritation are the film processors. Most (but not all) of the machines operate on a photographic principle and require developing just like camera film.[3] This means tanks of chemicals and washes, plus dry-

---

[2] A microfiche is a sheet of film with as many as one thousand or more "pages" of data reproduced on it in miniature form. You should be able to obtain samples from local suppliers. However, at least one supplier of the film offers samples to anyone who writes: Micrographics Division, GAF Corporation, 140 West 51st Street, New York, New York 10019.

[3] The COM recorder is manufactured by 3M Company. It is called the EBR, and it forms the image with an electron beam; the film is processed by another technique. Duplicates are frequently made using vesicular film, which is processed without any chemical baths.

ing, and, since the film is so long, these must be motorized—
like processing movie film. If you are going to be processing
this type of film, you are going to end up adding a technician,
or at least adding another technology to your operations.

An advantage of microfilm is the ease and economy of making multiple copies, whereby everyone who needs the information can have his or her own data and not have to go to a common file area to obtain printed volumes.

Together with the training of personnel, a COM installation
can represent an investment of several hundred thousand dollars. For this reason, and because of the great speed of the
machines, there is small justification for any company to acquire
its own COM machine unless it has a very high volume of
record keeping. Fortunately, there are ways in which smaller
companies, ones that could not justify installing their own COM
machine, can obtain access to one as needed.

First, there are service bureaus offering COM service, which
is how The Stuart McGuire Company, the subject of the case
history in Chapter 12, obtains its microfiche. Some of these
service bureaus are outgrowths of service organizations that
have long offered a variety of microfilm record conversions.
Others are newly organized around a COM machine, and only
offer that specialty in microfilming. How do you find such
services? Look in your local classified phone book, under Microfilming Service, Equipment and Supplies. Among the ads you
will find suppliers offering "COM service" or "mag tape to
microfilm." Make a list of such suppliers and check them out
carefully before scheduling a test run with the most likely
candidates.

There's another possible source: a local company with its
own underutilized COM machine. The company may not be

134

looking openly for outside business, but it might welcome additional work for the machine, even at break-even prices, just to help amortize its big investment.

How COM is used

What data should be converted from the computer's files onto microfiche or microfilm? In customer service installations, computerized records of customers' orders are the key documents—not the customer order itself. By checking the computer record of the order, the customer service clerk can answer a number of questions, such as:

When was the order processed?

Where was the merchandise shipped?

What specific items were transcribed from the customer order?

What item was not available and placed on back order?

What is the customer's open balance?

Errors in billing can be cleared up, too, by reference to the COM. The prices of the merchandise and the amount of merchandise sent to the customer can be checked for accuracy. (An illustration of a COM display is shown in Figure 24.)

CONCLUSION: AUTOMATION MUST BE COST-EFFECTIVE

By now my position on technology should be quite apparent: Apply new technology in customer relations—or in any aspect

FIGURE 24

ZIP	NAME	ADDRESS	ACCOUNT NUMBER	ORDER NUMBER	DATE	PAYMENT	QTY	ITEM	PRICE	AMOUNT	TAX	S&H	ORDER TOTAL
07861	NORTH RIVER A C BUTLER NJ	517 S SEVENTH ST	1351576	530910271	11/08/5		1	13714	5.95	5.95			
							1	15198	10.50	10.50			
										15.45		2.50	17.95
				PAYMENT	11/29/5	17.95						BALANCE	.00
	ARTHUR WALKER	RR 2	2157113	530702158	11/04/5		1	08714	17.95	17.95			
										17.95		1.00	18.95
				PAYMENT	11/20/5	18.95						BALANCE	.00
07862	OLDTOWN ROBERT GREGORY NJ	15 WASHINGTON ST	0165514	532827011	11/25/5		2	05546	7.95	15.90			
										15.90		2.00	17.90
				PAYMENT	11/25/5	17.90						BALANCE	.00
	ELSA LOWELL	11 ELM PLACE	3771516	PAYMENT	11/04/5	15.30							
				531731172	11/14/5		1	03133	4.95	B/O			
							1	15198	10.50	10.50			
										10.50		1.50	12.00
												BALANCE	12.00

A COM (computer output microfilm) display showing details of orders and payments. The customers' names are alphabetically arranged within zipcode areas.

of business operations—where it is *cost-effective*. On the other hand, applying new technology for its own sake, or to enhance the company's image, is not only silly and expensive but could actually result in slower and less effective responses to customers.

chapter 10

Efficient use of national network for telephone inquiries

The chauffeur of an 80-foot tractor-trailer rig moving at 55 miles per hour down a dark highway he has never traveled before is dismayed to hear a strange sound welling up from the engine compartment behind his seat. Within a few seconds, the high-torque diesel engine starts to lose power and the driver inches the big rig over to the side of the road.

The experienced driver first lights flares to warn the drivers of oncoming vehicles about the presence of his machine, then he walks back a few hundred yards to a home he spotted just as the diesel began to falter. The homeowner, responding to the driver's courteous request, permits him to place a call to an "800" number that was pasted inside the cab. Within a few seconds, the driver knows the phone number of the nearest open garage that can service his stricken machine. This has to be nearly the ultimate in responding to a cry for help from a customer.

The first use of the telephone to communicate with a business most likely occurred the first day a phone was installed for commercial purposes. In other words, about 100 years ago. The regular use of the phone to communicate between customer and supplier was implemented by the appearance of telephone directories. (The first was issued by New Haven District Telephone Company of Connecticut in 1878; it was one page long and listed 21 subscribers.)

However, it was the publication of classified phone books that formalized doing business by phone. The first "yellow pages" containing business advertising was issued on April 1, 1906, by the Michigan State Telephone Company for Detroit.

Today, the vast majority of Americans routinely "let their fingers do the walking." In 1969 the Bell Telephone System did a survey of shopping by phone and found that of those who used the Yellow Pages, 89 percent followed up with some action, not necessarily placing an order.

The "89 percent" figure has been appropriated by the companies offering inward-WATS lines for hire. Everyone who watches television, listens to the radio, or reads newspapers or magazines is aware of the availability of "800" numbers for voice transmission of orders or of requests for information. Some of the companies offering their "800" numbers for selling have made the claim that "89 percent of Americans use '800' numbers." This sounds to me like one of those statistics that gains credence because it is quoted so frequently.

However, it appears evident that more and more Americans and Canadians,[1] too, will use inward-WATS lines for placing orders, or for obtaining required information. The appeal to the seller is simple—a single number, rather than many, can be promoted (at the very least this simplifies TV commercials where local numbers must be inserted by card). The appeal to

---

[1] Listfax "Order Phone" service has an exchange in Toronto. Canadians cannot dial toll free on inward-WATS lines in the United States.

the buyer is also obvious—he or she does not have to pay for the phone call or a stamp on a mail order.

No one knows how much of the estimated $50 billion in mail-and-phone-order business for 1975 was done by phone. For instance, there are reports that over half of the approximately $2 billion done annually by Sears in catalog sales is now received by phone.

However, the level of orders received by phone is certainly in the billions and sure to grow fast. As a result, problems and customer complaints will arise. So we should be aware of the way in which orders are received by phone and how problems can arise.

Giant operations, like those of Sears and Ward, usually employ their own operators to accept orders received by mail, and at any hour of day or night. However, there is a growing trend towards use of specialized services for this purpose. The appeal of these services is obvious. First, because they are specialists, they presumably know how to handle these orders, and how best to select and train operators. Second, the operators can be hired just to cover a specific promotion, or to test out receipt of orders by phone. Finally, for a concern with offices in a downtown area, all problems associated with protection of company facilities and personnel after hours are eliminated. Imagine trying to recruit operators to man the phones in a large empty building in a deserted downtown area for the midnight to 8 A.M. shift on a Sunday morning!

SHARED OR DEDICATED INWARD-WATS LINES?

The half-dozen or so organizations (they are listed in an appendix at the end of this chapter) that offer "800" numbers for order collection provide these lines of communication on two bases: dedicated and shared. If you expect a heavy volume of order taking on a continuing basis all year round, you might find that a "renting" of numbers exclusive to your company makes sense. When a potential customer calls one of these dedicated "800" numbers, the operator answers with your company name.

If you are merely testing the applicability of "800" numbers to your product and do not expect a heavy volume of orders, or if you are offering a seasonal product or a one-shot deal, then it makes sense to share an "800" number with other clients of the telecommunications service. When a potential customer calls a shared number, the operator answers with some nondistinguishing phrase, such as "Order Desk." Obviously, the operator must quickly find out which of many products offered on that number is of interest to the caller. There is a higher minimum charge for a dedicated line than a shared one, presumably, although the cost per order should be lower with a dedicated line if a high volume of orders is received. For example, one service charges a minimum of $500 per month for a shared line, but $1,500 is the minimum for a dedicated line. However, Mardex Corporation, which only offers dedicated lines, claims that they cost no more than shared lines.

In most instances for both dedicated and shared "800" numbers, the order information is taken down on small two-part order forms stacked in pigeonholes in front of each operator. In addition to the product of interest, the form usually carries one line indicating where the customer learned of the product (so the advertiser can quickly find out where best to advertise). If the product is to be paid by credit card, the operator can check the validity of that card within a few seconds over an outward-WATS line. Another group of employees "keyboard" the order forms onto a single computer tape for rapid transmittal over phone lines at low night rates right into the client's computer.

COMPUTER KEEPS TRACK OF INVENTORY OF OFFERINGS

A growing trend in this form of selling is to place the order forms in a computer memory, to be called up by the operator on her cathode-ray tube terminal. The form is displayed on the CRT unit in split seconds. All the operator has to do is fill in the blanks. Once the transaction has been completed, the operator merely hits one key and the transaction is automatically transferred from the screen of the terminal to the computer, thus eliminating the separate keyboarding operation required with the manual collection of orders. Also, the computer can keep track of inventory, warning the seller when stocks are low, as well as informing the order desk operator when the desired item is out of stock or if certain colors or other variations are out of stock. The computer could also check the customer's credit card number automatically and quickly, without requiring the operator to make a separate call on an outward-WATS line.

The orders can be transmitted to the seller in various ways: on paper, with accompanying labels carrying the customers' addresses; in the form of computer tape, which is sent by courier; and on tape transmitted over phone lines at night when the rates are lowest. If the seller so desires, the orders could be sent to the nearest designated retailer where the customer could pick up his purchase. Additionally, the results of the queries on the media by which the customers learned of the offer can be sent directly to the seller's ad agency. Instead of sending reports of credit card purchases just to the seller, these reports could go directly to the issuer of the credit or to a corresponding bank for immediate application of funds.

STOCKING BOTH MERCHANDISE AND MAGAZINES

Some of these services are even prepared to stock merchandise (as you can see below, they stock brochures) for shipment to customers. In a variation of this, Western Union and other services stock the latest issues of client magazines and forward just the first issue to new subscribers. In this way, a common subscriber complaint—"What's happened to my magazines; I subscribed weeks ago?"—is avoided. Or, the shipping labels could be sent to a warehouse for shipment of merchandise that is never handled by the seller.

Inevitably, once an "800" number becomes associated in the public's mind with a certain merchant, that merchant will receive complaints and other customer communications via those lines.

Some companies do not object to such queries. They pay the services to collect other communications than orders, and to forward them to the seller for action. Western Union, for example, which calls its service Response Phone, is only too happy to collect such reports at a standard rate of 65 cents per minute of operator time. On the other hand, many sellers and some of these services do not want to handle such communications, and the sellers print notices to this effect. For example, in its Fall/Winter 1975–1976 catalog, Bencone Uniforms of Westwood,

New Jersey, carries this notice on its order forms: "Important: Toll-free numbers are for placing orders only."

However, such a notice is not considered to be sufficient. Better to follow the guidance in the latest catalog from shirt-maker Lew Magram and provide the customer with an alternative number to call, if you wish to encourage customers to use the telephone to transmit complaints.

"800" NUMBERS NOT FOR CUSTOMER COMPLAINTS

Do *not* encourage the use of toll-free numbers for receipt of complaints. First of all, the volume of complaints received is sure to rise; in my experience, a 25 percent increase is to be expected. Since it costs money to answer complaints, any such increase may be considered undesirable. The second reason also involves money—these services charge for collection of complaints. And the duration of a call relating to a complaint could be quite lengthy. Let's assume that 2,000 complaints are received each month on toll-free lines, and that the average length of calls is two minutes. If the service charges only 65 cents per minute, the minimum cost per month is $2,600.

Instead of accepting complaints via "800" numbers, I urge companies to accept collect calls from irate customers.

SOLICITED CUSTOMER QUERIES

On the other hand, there is a category of customer communication that most companies are only too delighted to receive: a query for the name of the nearest dealer carrying that product. Dealer location is the way toll-free numbers actually began. For at least two decades, Western Union offered its Operator 25 service for this purpose. Those who called Western Union and asked for Operator 25 were informed of the name and address of the nearest dealer. These dealers were listed on sheets of paper.

By the late 1960s, the Operator 25 service had declined to a very low level. At this point, some entrepreneurs who had acted in an advisory capacity to Western Union came up with the idea of offering an updated version of Operator 25 on the inward-WATS lines then coming into use. At first, according to I. C. "Win" Roll, chairman of Listfax, the phone company was unhappy with the concept. It saw Listfax as a sort of common carrier, which meant that it had to be regulated. However, the concept was ultimately accepted by Ma Bell and the Federal Communications Commission did not become involved, and Listfax began operating in 1967. Dealer—or repair service—location is now much more sophisticated. Instead of looking up the locations on printed media, the names and addresses are flashed on the operator's terminal. The operator merely keys in the zip code number of the caller, and the locations appear in split seconds.

A competitor of Listfax, Dialog Marketing, has gone one step further. Callers are not only provided with the name and address of the nearest dealer or repair service, but its proximity to the caller as well.

ELIMINATING PROBLEMS

It's easy to see how problems can arise with telephone orders. First of all, the number of the credit card or the address of the buyer could be taken down erroneously. Next, the numbers of items ordered, if the situation involves a wide selection, could be transmitted or received erroneously. Finally, an inventory problem could arise because of unanticipated demand. The last is a very real problem: one of the Big Three carmakers offered a useful little brochure to the public via a toll-free number, which became inundated by the volume of callers, who soon exhausted the original print run of 250,000 copies.

To avoid errors in communicating a credit card number, those sellers who accept purchases via the cards urge their customers to make the call "with card in hand." Presumably, the account number can be read off the card correctly, and the caller can provide the correct address, with zip code. This admonition could also save money for sellers who pay by total of calls, because the customer doesn't have to hunt down his or her credit card after dialing the "800" number.

To avoid problems with item numbers where a multiplicity of products is offered, sellers should emulate Sears and other major mail-order merchants and include a "phone order planner" with their catalogs (see Figure 25). Thus, the customer can quickly read off the items, the catalog numbers, color, size, and price—holding down on phone charges for the seller—and the customer can also retain the planner as a record of his or her purchases in the event some question arises later. But follow the Sears' procedure and prominently display on the planner the following injunction: "This form is only for your convenience —please do not mail it in."

The inventory problem is a tougher one to overcome. The seller has to establish some means of keeping track of items offered, of reordering quickly if the order volume indicates a higher than anticipated demand, and of telling the service pro-

146

FIGURE 25

PAGE NO.	CATALOG NUMBER	HOW MANY	NAME OF ITEM	COLOR Pattern, Finish, Etc	SIZE Measure to be sure	PRICE Ea., Yd., Pr., Etc	TOTAL PRICE Dollars	Cents	SHPG. WT. Lbs	Oz

DATE ORDERED	DATE TO BE PICKED UP	TOTAL

You can use this Planner to write down
all the necessary information on items
you wish to order. Refer to it when you call us
and, afterward, you'll have a written record.

Here's how to use this form:

- When you find an item you wish to order, jot
  down all the information in the spaces on the form.
- Phone in your order with all the information
  right in front of you ... no need to thumb through
  the book again.
- Refer to this form when items are delivered to make
  sure you received the color, size, etc. you ordered.
- This form is only for your convenience—please
  do not mail it in.

Phone Number of your nearest
Sears Catalog selling unit:

My Sears Credit Card number:

WANT A SEARS CREDIT CARD?
Just mention it when you call
and we'll take your application
by phone

F55016 4 74

The Sears "phone order planner" and its detailed instructions for use.

viding the "800" numbers when a given item is no longer available or not available in certain colors or sizes.

In clothing and other industries, where there is a long lead time involved in manufacture of merchandise, the operator has no choice but to inform the caller, "The item you wish is now out of stock." However, what if the seller is in a position to reorder? Does it make sense to instruct the operators to accept orders with this stipulation: "We are temporarily out of stock on this item due to high demand, but we will have it available for shipment in about four weeks"?

Experience has shown that the phone callers would not accept as long a delay in delivery of merchandise ordered by phone as they would when ordering by mail.

There is still another action that could be taken by the operator. Instead of ending the conversation with no sale, why not offer the customer something else, or offer the same item in another color? The services train their operators to engage in a bit of selling when the client so requests. Cards with short, snappy "sell" copy can be mounted in front of each operator. Or, if the operator is equipped with a computer terminal, "sell" copy that has been memorized by the computer could be flashed in front of the operator.

HOW DO THESE SERVICES CHARGE?

There are two basic ways in which these services charge: by duration of call or by the order. Western Union charges only by duration of call and, as indicated earlier, the charge is a flat 65 cents per minute. The service organizations that are oriented to order gathering generally charge by the order. An estimate is made of the average length of order, then the per-order charge is based on this estimate. Other charges are associated with the service. Dialog Marketing, which has created a "rate card" similar to that of advertising media has various charges beyond the basic time or per-order charge.

These charges include: the initial account set-up, which is a one-time $200 charge; the dealer file set-up, a one-time charge for inserting into the computer each dealer's name at ten cents apiece (this includes a monthly computer printout, in duplicate, of each dealer file); and the dealer file maintenance, which is a monthly charge of three cents each plus 35 cents for each update ($25 per month minimum). Listfax's charges for dealer referral are based on the circulation of the publications in which the "800" number is given.

"DEALER ALERT"

Besides informing clients of the names of customers who query about dealer locations, these services will also inform that nearest dealer or agent about the inquiry. Dialog Marketing charges 45 cents apiece for mailing a postcard that indicates the customer interest by product, plus his address. If these post-cards, which are supposed to be mailed daily, are not expeditious enough, Dialog Marketing will alert the dealer or agent by Mailgram or direct-dial phone call at charges ranging from 90 cents to $2.50 per communication.

INFORMATION SERVICES

In addition to all of the above, some of these services provide useful information on a toll-free basis. For instance, Listfax provided detailed information on a new drug via a recording. If the physician calling the number wanted more information (presumably only professional people were aware of this service), he or she was given the phone number of a specialist who could answer the questions.

Some experts are looking ahead to the day when computers will be able to understand questions posed by callers (the experts call this speech recognition) and provide answers by a speech-generating apparatus. Although this development is still far off in the future, economically if not technically, it does indicate the direction in which these services are heading. Obviously, they have a big role to play in customer communications.

SELLING BY OUTWARD-WATS

Selling by phone is not confined to inward-WATS lines, which, incidentally, are not available in Alaska and Hawaii, just in the 48 contiguous states and Canada. Selling by outward-WATS lines is also increasing, but on a much lower scale. Instead of mailing an offering to a potential customer, the prospect is called on the phone. If the publication, product, or service is for a personal use, the customer is usually called at home in the evening. However, if the offering is for a business or professional use, the call comes during business hours.

The original purpose of unsolicited selling by phone was to raise funds for political campaigns. However, when the man who claims to be the originator of such organized selling, Murray Roman, realized its potential, he founded a company devoted to this purpose, Campaign Communications Institute of America, Inc., 641 Lexington Avenue, New York, New York 10022. Roman speaks of his technique as one that makes the telephone a medium of advertising.

Selling in this manner is done in two ways. Either the calling operator reads a rehearsed message to the party who has been called, or a short recorded pitch is played to the receptive party at the other end. Roman claims that his service generated a substantial subscription list for Norman Cousins's then unborn *World* magazine by playing a tape recording of Cousins describing his new publication many, many months before the first issue was published.

Since this new form of selling does not provide the customer with a number to query, it would not play much of a role in customer complaints or other communications.

APPENDIX

Dialog Marketing, Inc.   1909 E. Cornell, Peoria, Ill. 61614 and 15 West 44th Street, New York, New York 10036.

Information Management, Inc.   9124 Bedford Avenue, Omaha, Nebraska 68134.

Listfax Corporation.   1370 Avenue of the Americas, New York, New York 10019.

Mardex Corporation.   60 East 42nd Street, New York, New York 10017, and 9105 Bedford Avenue, Omaha, Nebraska 68134.

National Order Systems, Inc.   2 West 45th Street, New York, New York 10036.

Western Union.   One Lake Street, Upper Saddle River, New Jersey 07458.

chapter 11

Outside help

Every successful business depends to some extent on help from outsiders. This aid may be as simple as ideas picked up from trade publications, or as suggestions gleaned during informational meetings with salesmen and customers. The people who benefit from such unprogrammed inputs may not even be aware that they are soliciting ideas from outsiders, or they may have such colossal egos that their unconscious denies that they are depending occasionally on others for useful concepts. However, there is no denying the dependence upon intelligence from outside their own organizations.

In setting policy for and operating a customer service function, companies are well advised to seek help from outsiders for three good reasons:

A. There are many governmental agencies operating in consumer affairs (no less than 35 agencies in the federal government alone). Executives responsible for this function are likely to either waste a lot of time trying to keep informed or remain ignorant of some important new legislation or regulation. To avoid such problems, they should subscribe to an information service (see Chapter 3) or participate in an association devoted to gathering and presenting new information in this fast-evolving field.

B. For competitive reasons, responsible executives should be aware of practices in competing or similar companies. This is to insure that their company's level of response does not fall so far behind that damage is done either in lowered sales or in damaging publicity as a result of a citation from a consumer advocate.

C. The operation of a customer service function is quite specialized, and the part-time executive is likely to organize it in a way that costs too much. For example, executives not versed in customer communications greatly *overestimate* the need for formality in responding to customers. Formality is costly and usually is slower than quite acceptable informality.

SOURCES FOR HELP IN CUSTOMER COMMUNICATIONS

Five main outside sources of help and counsel are available to executives who are responsible for customer service and communications:

1. Knowledgeable executives in local and supplier companies.
2. Your trade association.
3. Professional organizations devoted to consumer affairs.
4. Consumer affairs departments in local government.
5. Consultants.

Knowledgeable outside executives

Neophytes in consumer affairs are well advised to seek aid and counsel from their counterparts in local businesses and among suppliers. As is true of most such executives, they should be quite willing to counsel others at no charge. (An occasional luncheon might be all that is required to return the favor.) Most will be highly flattered that you're asking for their advice. The consumer affairs specialist with a supplier company should feel it his duty to advise the executives of customer companies. Once you've established a healthy relationship with such an expert, you should be able to phone him occasionally for aid with problems. These experts also should be able to recommend reliable local sources for whatever hardware and paper supplies are needed in a customer service department.

Trade association role in consumer affairs

More and more trade associations are developing programs to help their members cope with the growing problem of customer service.[1] If you are not aware that your own national or regional trade association has such a program, just call the executive director and ask him or her what help the association offers in this expanding field. Even if the association does not have a formally organized function in consumer affairs, the executive director may be able to advise members on practices in the industry. Additionally, he should be able to refer those persons seeking aid to counterparts in other companies that belong to the association.

---

[1] There are so many trade associations offering help in consumer affairs that the Chamber of Commerce compiled in 1973 a directory of 90 of them and what they do for members in this field. The directory, *Association Consumer Affairs Activities,* is available at $4 each from: Chamber of Commerce of the United States, 1615 H Street, N.W., Washington, D.C. 20006. The 56-page directory also contains an order list of publications available from the chamber to aid concerned executives. Many are available gratis in single-copy quantities.

Professional organizations in consumer affairs

The leading association devoted entirely to consumer affairs is SOCAP—the Society of Consumer Affairs Professionals in Business. Organized in 1973, this specialized association consists of some 400 members, mostly from larger companies. Although the members are nearly all executives whose major responsibility in a great variety of companies is consumer affairs, some members have part-time duties in this field, and the program of the society is indeed of value to part-timers and those in smaller companies.

The best way to comprehend the function of SOCAP is to simply reprint its statement of purpose:

The Society of Consumer Affairs Professionals in Business shall foster the integrity of business in its dealings with consumers, promote harmonious relationships between business and government and consumers, and advance the consumer affairs profession.

SOCAP publishes a bimonthly newsletter reporting developments in consumer affairs, organizes seminars on specific subjects of wide interest, and conducts national and regional meetings of its members. The seminars and meetings draw as speakers and participants the experts and governmental executives with whom the individual executive is hardly likely to come in contact. For example, at the Western Regional Meeting held in May 1974, one of the speakers was Barbara Hackman Franklin, vice chairman of the Consumer Products Safety Commission of the federal government.

Regular membership in SOCAP costs $60 per year; however, an associate membership, which is nonvoting, costs $30 per year. For information on membership and SOCAP activities, write to the society at 1750 Old Meadow Road, McLean, Virginia 22101, (703) 893–7761.

Beside SOCAP, a number of trade associations are cutting across industry lines with a heavy emphasis on customer service. These are: the Direct Mail/Marketing Association, Inc. (DMMA), 6 East 43rd Street, New York, New York 10017, (212) 689–4977; the Direct Selling Association, 1730 M Street, N.W., Suite 610, Washington, D.C. 20036, (202) 293–5760; and The Conference Board, 845 Third Avenue, New York, New York 10022, (212) 759–0900.

In addition to these, the National Retail Merchants Association (NRMA), 100 West 31st Street, New York, New York, (212) 244–8780, informs its members of important developments in consumer affairs relating to the retail merchant.

As an example of what these organizations do in consumer affairs, the DMMA has been conducting one-day conferences in New York and Chicago that are devoted solely to the problems of handling customer communications. It also has sponsored for more than a dozen years an annual Government Affairs Conference, which is always held in Washington. At one recent two-day conference, a number of important questions were discussed. Among them were: "Will rental and exchange of mailing lists continue to be allowed?" and "What new rules and guidelines from the powerful Consumer Product Safety Commission will affect you?"

Seeking aid from consumer advocates

It may appear to some individuals to be trafficking with the enemy to approach consumer advocates for aid in solving problems in customer relations. And would these strong supporters of consumerism help businessmen? The answer is seen in programs of SOCAP and other organizations promoting good customer relations. Over and over again, consumer advocates are invited to and address such meetings. Obviously, they relish talking shop with their opposite numbers in business. In other words, they are not so much "antibusiness" as opposed to deficiencies in the way business deals with its customers. By promoting proper practices in relations with consumers, these advocates are actually *helping* the business community.

Of course, there are some radical types who are climbing on the bandwagon of consumerism to find yet another platform for their diatribes. But such extremists are very much in the minority. Most of the many consumer advocates are reasonable people who want to get their point of view across to businessmen. Most are very articulate and only too willing to sit down with businessmen and "rap."

So take advantage of the open door policy of consumer advocates in your locality and engage in fruitful dialogs with them. You will not only gain useful information but you might blunt some future adverse publicity release. Consumer advocates are not likely to rush to denounce a company whose executives appear honest and open to reasonable suggestions.

There is one consumer advocate that is known to welcome inquiries for help from businessmen—the Better Business Bureau. In many instances your company need not be a member of your local BBB to ask for advice and counsel on customer relations.

When consultants are needed

Much valuable information can be gleaned from the four sources of help mentioned above. However, the company with special or serious problems in customer communications may have to turn to a more high-powered source of help. Two of the prime reasons why companies engage consultants and cannot rely on less-formal sources are *confidentiality* and *objectivity*. Those who proffer or are dependent upon "free" advice are not as well motivated to maintain secrecy as is the consultant who depends for his bread and butter on his integrity and ability to hold completely confidential a serious problem revealed to him by a client. (More later on other criteria for choosing a consultant.)

The "outside eye" looking in also provides an impartial and fresh viewpoint. A consultant sees the whole picture and frequently spots and resolves problems where management cannot be truly objective. Further, since the consultant is not selling specific equipment or services, he is in a position to evaluate fairly the suggestions originating within the company and from outside salesmen.

The consultant also has the time available to delve into a problem because he's hired by the day or hour. And a serious, costly problem may take more than a few hours or few days to resolve. In addition, the experienced consultant may be more aware of the latest trends in customer service than is a local source.

Here are just a few examples of what a consultant can do for your customer service function: to tell you whether you are performing satisfactorily or poorly, and, if poorly, help you "get organized"; to recommend new and modern systems, procedures, and equipment; to evaluate your present personnel; to counsel you on what policies to follow; and to train your supervision.

When company "politics" calls for a consultant. Sometimes companies call in a consultant to resolve a problem because of company politics rather than because someone inside the company can't solve it. Although experienced consultants are aware that they are brought into the situation for "political" reasons, they never let this weaker but nevertheless valid motivation distract them from doing their best for the client.

For example, a consultant recently was called in to resolve a "communications" problem of a major manufacturing corporation. The company systems engineer, who engaged the services of the organization, did indeed have a good insight into just how one high executive's office was fouled up. However, he did not have enough authority to "counsel" this executive on his deficiencies. In this particular situation, the deficient executive was able to swallow the consultant's recommendation with much greater ease than if it had originated with a middle-management executive. Additionally, the consultant went beyond the system engineer's assessment of the situation to suggest other viable ways to successfully resolve the situation.

Better hardware solutions.   One of the valuable functions of consultants is to steer clients from overly costly or extremely clumsy hardware that adds to, rather than ameliorates, a communications problem. (Earlier in Chapter 9, opinions are offered—based on direct experience—dealing with problems associated with some of the costly systems that have been employed in customer communications.) Because the active consultant spends all his time going from one client's facility to another, he should be aware of which equipment works well and which is not cost-effective, or which is encumbered with serious deficiencies, either in design, capacity, or service. It is in this area of equipment recommendations that fees paid to consultants can really pay off. Where the equipment cost is very high, as in the case of computer systems, avoidance of a mistake not only saves hundreds of thousands of dollars but also permits the client to implement the better (and usually less costly) solution in much less time.

SELLING THE NEW CONCEPT
TO THE COMPANY

There's still another way in which consultants can perform yeoman service for clients. Once a plan for a new approach to customer service has been developed, it has to be "sold" to the employees who must implement it. The consultant who developed the plan, in collaboration with company executives, may be better qualified to present it to skeptical clerks, who are likely to see the new concept as a threat to their jobs or as some form of "speedup." A well-thought-out plan for improving customer service enriches the jobs of those who implement it, and makes them *more valuable* to the company.

Because she or he has been through the process so many times, the experienced consultant should be able to anticipate all the objections or the hidden animosities of employees affected by the new approach, then resolve them in an intelligent manner. In contrast, a company executive, who has little experience in getting a radically new system off the ground, may try to implement it by the weight of authority alone.

How to pick a consultant

Because there are so many management consulting firms (about 3,500 at last count in the United States alone), and many more individuals who call themselves management consultants, the choice of one capable of resolving problems in customer service could be a chore. This is where contacts with other company specialists in this field, your trade association, or participation in SOCAP is a big help. Inquiries that are made at one or more of these sources, or to Philip Shay, executive director of the Association of Consulting Management Engineers (ACME), 347 Madison Avenue, New York, New York 10017, (212) 686-7338, should reveal the names of consultants who are qualified in this special aspect of business.

Once you have compiled a list of such qualified consultants, this is the procedure you should follow: Ask each consultant to submit a written proposal that covers these five aspects of the project:

1. Objectives and the consultant's approach to achieve them.
2. Results that could be expected from the study.
3. Probable length of time required, plus the estimated professional fees and attendant expenses.
4. Particular experience and ability of the staff consultants who are likely to be assigned to complete the project.
5. The form in which the final report will be made.

In addition, ask each consultant interviewed to include the following information with her or his proposal: number of years in business; background and experience of the principals and staff members; types of client; and the amount and extent of repeat business.

Don't hesitate to ask for client references from the consultants whose proposals deserve serious consideration. Telephone the key contact at each reference and ask them these questions:

Were the consultant's recommendations timely, practical, and suited to the needs of the client?

How well did the consultants work with the client's personnel, from executives down to workers? In particular, were
they able to implement their recommendations when they
were asked to do so, with a minimum of friction and
resentment?

Was the job done within the estimated time? Or, if the
estimate was exceeded substantially, was this due to the
consultant's underestimation of the job or because the
client expanded its scope (which often happens)?

Finally, would the client hire that consultant again for
similar work?

If selecting the proper consultant sounds like a big chore,
remember that you're trying to locate a *resource* that not only
will help you solve present problems but future ones as well.
In choosing a consultant, don't be misled by any so-called management consultant who *guarantees* savings in operational cost
or time, or who proposes to charge a fee only if results are
obtained. These are touchstones of unprofessional practice.

CONCLUSION: NO MONOPOLY ON BRAINS

What has been emphasized in this chapter is the notion that
no one has a monopoly on "smarts."

In customer service and communications, as in any other
aspect of business, the successful organization draws on suitable
resources both within and without the company.

chapter 12

A successful updating of customer relations

Annual savings of over $40,000—mostly as a result of a customer service staff reduction from 20 to 12.

Responding to almost all communications in two days—instead of within three weeks.

Achieving both of these goals with a small investment is what makes the upgrading of customer service at The Stuart McGuire Company such an instructive case history.

The Stuart McGuire Company, which is located in Salem, Virginia, is a direct seller of men's and women's shoes and clothing, and recently expanded into linens and bed coverings. Incorporated in 1926, the company is now publicly held and does about $30 million in sales each year. All sales are handled by its over 180,000 independent, part-time sales personnel, who sell by means of attractive, profusely illustrated catalogs. The four-color catalogs are published in two versions twice a year.

Since many of the 500 phone calls and letters received each working day come from the company's sales representatives, it is obviously important to respond promptly and accurately. Recognizing that its customer service was not up to snuff, management began in 1971 to seek ways to upgrade the system that had grown like Topsy over the years.

One of the management's first moves was to order a $25,000 microfilm retrieval system to speed the looking up of customer orders. Shortly thereafter, Fenvessy Associates, Inc., the New York-based consulting firm of which the author is president, was invited to propose an upgrading of the system. About six weeks later, in August 1971, a detailed plan was submitted to management suggesting many ways in which customer service could be improved. Included in this 55-page report was the recommendation that the planned microfilm retrieval system *not* be implemented. Ultimately, the unused equipment was returned to the supplier at only a modest loss.

Key recommendations

Many recommendations were in the report, but the key ones, those to which the great gain in productivity could be ascribed, are as follows:

1. Organizing the work force into three-person teams was the first step, each team consisting of a team leader, senior clerk, and trainee. Four such teams were set up initially, but they proved so productive that within nine months only three were required. The nation is broken down into large regions, with one team assigned to each. Records of productivity are maintained for each team.

2. A method was set up of quickly picking out mail containing complaints from salesmen (the great majority of representatives are male). The report recommended renting a separate post office box for such communications, but management opted for distinctively colored envelopes addressed to the com-

pany, and this method of segregating complaints has proven adequate. (Most of the complaints from customers are forwarded via the salesmen, who are themselves substantial purchasers of company products.)

3. Mail is carefully sorted by region and complexity. In common with other successful customer service groups, the best people, not the newly hired, are assigned to sorting. Within each team, the most complex complaints are assigned to the most experienced team member.

4. A colored date indicator is stapled to each letter as it is removed from its envelope. Color tagging helps insure that each day's mail is completed before the work on the next day's correspondence is begun. (A detailed discussion of date indicators is presented in Chapter 8.)

5. To simplify and speed the process of checking the status of a customer's order, current order and shipping information is prepared on microfiche—four-inch by six-inch sheets of film containing 204 pages of computer printout photographically reduced by a factor of 42. Each team is provided with two microfiche readers and two complete sets of microfiche. Looking up data on the microfiche takes about 30 percent less time than the former method of checking large, bound, and bulky volumes of computer printout. (More details later on the microfiche.)

6. Each day an average of 75 phone inquiries are received from salesmen or customers. By means of the microfiche, most complaints can be resolved quickly while the party is on the line.

7. "Decision tables" have been created to guide the sales service clerks in seeking the correct response to an inquiry, and in consistent application of adjustment policies.

8. A packing slip is included in each shipment; the slip contains all of the information needed to handle an adjustment transaction. This information provides the customer's name and address, order number, description of merchandise ordered, and shipping date. On the reverse side are instructions on how to return the merchandise; under this are boxes to check to indi-

FIGURE 26

Front of form

Back of form

Packing slip provided by the Stuart McGuire Company to assist customers in exchanging merchandise for a better fit.

166

cate what the problem was and what should be done (see Figure 26).

Fast responses—through informality

To speed the process of responding, clerks have been instructed to handwrite responses on simplified-form postcards or letters. (Among the short tests taken by all clerks is one for legible handwriting.) Thus, the effort and delay previously devoted to dictating, transcribing, and typing letters is eliminated. Only the most complex complaints, making up less than ten percent of all responses, require formal replies. Previously, 52 percent of all complaints were replied to in a formal manner. Both salespersons and customers accept the informal approach.

To further speed up responses, mail is collected before the end of the day and delivered to the post office in time to meet local dispatch schedules.

Why microfiche?

It should be apparent that the great gains in higher productivity and faster response are mainly the result of reorganization, careful selection of personnel, explicit definition of service policies, and the use of such very simple and low-cost techniques as packing slips and color tagging. Advanced technology plays only a small role. Nevertheless, for anyone unfamiliar with microfilming techniques, a discussion of the process by which the microfiche are created should be instructive.

The information displayed on the microfiche is that which has been recorded on the magnetic tapes associated with the company's in-house computer. The actual orders received from salesmen are merely batched in groups of 50 and filed, after the information on them has been entered into the computer by means of a key-to-disk data entry system. Only rarely do the sales service clerks refer to these original orders.

Once a week, magnetic tapes duplicating those on which all order data are stored are sent to a service bureau in Greensboro, North Carolina, about 100 miles from the headquarters of The Stuart McGuire Company. This bureau operates a COM (computer output microfilm) recorder, a costly, complex contraption that directly transcribes the magnetic information on the tapes into microfiche, without an intermediate creation of pages of paper. The data on the magnetic tape is transcribed onto sheets of microfiche, and then ten copies of each microfiche are made on high-speed duplicating machines at the bureau.

At the time of the original proposal, it was calculated that the cost per "page" of information on microfiche, including three copies, was only $0.054. This was only two tenths of a cent more than the hard-copy presentation of the same pages of data used previously, and much less costly than to create the data in original and three duplicates in hard copy.

Some investment was required to convert to microfiche, but this was only $4,000 for programming and for nine microfiche viewers. (The particular brand and model of viewer is not revealed here because we have found that there are many satisfactory viewers on the market, ranging in cost from $150 to $200.) This one-time $4,000 investment was more than recouped in savings in personnel, in computer printing time, and in paper costs.

Employee reaction "enthusiastic"

How did the sales service clerks react to the switch from hard copy to microfiche? "Enthusiastically," is the only way to describe their response. Previously, in many cases, they had to get up from their stations to refer to the hard-copy compilation of order and shipping data. They also have found that the microfiche is actually more legible than the computer printed copy.

In fact, the new system has been enthusiastically received by the clerks on all counts. Employees will always prefer a system in which their tasks are well defined, and by which their output can be measured. Conversely, when jobs are poorly defined, and there is no way in which the lazy can be singled out from the productive, employees are not as happy and their collective output goes down.

Another achievement of the new system has been the upgrading of a supervisor to that of manager of the sales service function, with the reassignment of the previous manager.

Savings twice as high as anticipated

In the original proposal, first-year savings of $21,350 were projected, with annual savings thereafter at $25,350, because the $4,000 investment to implement microfiche was only required in the first year. Actual savings have been on the order of double the projected savings, in large part because of the reduction in duplicate complaints resulting from the quicker and more accurate responses to the salesman's or customer's first inquiry.

However, the real return from the improved system cannot be measured in dollars. Secondary to Direct Marketing Consultant, Robert D. Kestnbaum, customer goodwill and enthusiasm on the part of salesmen are vital to a direct selling operation like The Stuart McGuire Company. Fast, accurate responses help sustain these vital intangibles.

Index